Praise for Michael E. Gerber, Austin Clark, and *The E-Myth Pest Control Business*

Imagine a toolkit designed to make your business 'turnkey' and supercharge growth! Austin Clark's commitment to operational excellence and scalability is evident. Take it from someone who has 'been there.' Austin's insights will catapult you past the competition.

Verne Harnish, *Founder Entrepreneurs' Organization (EO) and author of Scaling Up (Rockefeller Habits 2.0)*

Over the years I have talked to thousands of owners, entrepreneurs, and CEO's. I consider Austin to be a trusted source anywhere from leadership, to management, to pricing to attracting your customers to marketing. He is the whole package, and his book is the whole package. I go back to Austin to learn over and over, lesson and fundamentals, fundamentals I need to be reminded of. Thank you, Austin for creating such a treasure trove of a book that myself and everyone else can learn from.

Dr. Jeremy Weisz, Cofounder of Rise25

I first met Austin over a decade ago, and quite frankly, I've never known anyone like him. He's always been an advocate for the Home Service Industry - genuine, truthful, poised, and willing to help anyone. Further, his operations run with smooth, machine-like precision. People literally line up to work with him, but now he's passing on his wisdom to everyone through this amazing book!"

Tommy Mello, CEO of A1 Garage Door Service and
author of Home Service Millionaire

Austin is providing those of us working in the pest control service industry, with great foundational guidance every owner needs to put into practice to be able to transition from a technician (under $1M) working in the business and then manager (under $5M) still working in the business and ultimately to an independent advisor working on the business with little daily operational responsibility. Austin does a great job of clearing the work noise and provides his audience with clear steps to make small daily changes which over time provide exceptional results. There were so many situations that Austin shares that I directly experienced and I wonder what it would have been like to know this early on in my career. Things would have happened so much faster and easier if I had known and now you can. Enjoy the read."

Scott Steckel, NPMA President, Plunkett's Pest Control
and Varment Guard Wildlife Services Strategic Development Director

"80% of the problem with most CEOs is they don't do enough deep thinking. Austin has done the deep thinking and laid out a thoughtful plan in plain language.....it all matters! You would be a near fool to not want to pour over these pages and turn your business from a living into a life!

Paul Akers, Author - 2 Second Lean

While there are no shortcuts to building a thriving and valuable pest control business, there are a lot of roadblocks to doing so. In The E-Myth Pest Control Business, Austin Clark systematically removes those roadblocks one by one, starting with you. This book is mandatory reading for any business owner who wants to get out of their own way and come on top in an industry that is getting more competitive by the minute.

Paul Giannamore, Managing Director, The Potomac Company

Michael Gerber's *E-Myth* is one of only four books I recommend as required reading. **For those looking to start and build a business of their own, this is the man who has coached more successful entrepreneurs than the next ten gurus combined.**

Timothy Ferris, #1 *New York Times* best-selling author,
The 4-Hour Workweek

Everyone needs a mentor, someone who tells it like it is, holds you accountable, and shows you your good, bad, and ugly. For millions of small business owners, Michael Gerber is that person. Let Michael be your mentor and you are in for a kick in the pants, the ride of a lifetime.

John Jantsch, author, *Duct Tape Marketing*

Michael Gerber is a master instructor and a leader's leader. As a combat F15 fighter pilot, I had to navigate complex missions with life-and-death consequences, but until I read *The E-Myth* and met Michael Gerber, my transition to the world of small business was a nightmare with no real flight plan. **The hands-on, practical magic of Michael's turnkey systems magnified by the raw power of his keen insight and wisdom have changed my life forever.**

Steve Olds, CEO, Stratworx.com

Michael Gerber's strategies in *The E-Myth* were instrumental in building my company from two employees to a global organization; I can't wait to see how applying the strategies from *Awakening the Entrepreneur Within* will affect its growth!

Dr. Ivan Misner, founder and chairman, BNI; author, *Masters of Sales*

Michael Gerber's gift to isolate the issues and present simple, direct, business-changing solutions shines bright with *Awakening the Entrepreneur Within*. If you're interested in developing an entrepreneurial vision and plan that inspires others to action, buy this book, read it, and apply the processes Gerber brilliantly defines.

Tim Templeton, author, *The Referral of a Lifetime*

Michael Gerber truly, truly understands what it takes to be a successful practicing entrepreneur and business owner. He has demonstrated to me over six years of working with him that for those who stay the course and learn much more than just "how to work on their business and not in it" then they will reap rich rewards. I finally franchised my business, and the key to unlocking this kind of potential in any business is the teachings of Michael's work.

Chris Owen, marketing director, Royal Armouries (International) PLC

Michael's work has been an inspiration to us. His books have helped us get free from the out-of-control life that we once had. His no-nonsense approach kept us focused on our ultimate aim rather than day-to-day stresses. He has helped take our business to levels we couldn't have imagined possible. In the Dreaming Room made us totally reevaluate how we thought about our business and our life. We have now redesigned our life so we can manifest the dreams we unearthed in Michael's Dreaming Room.

Jo and Steve Davison, founders, The Spinal Health Clinic Chiropractic Group and www.your-dream-life.com

Michael Gerber is an outrageous revolutionary who is changing the way the world does business. He dares you to commit to your grandest dreams and then shows you how to make the impossible a reality. If you let him, this man will change your life.

Fiona Fallon, founder, Divine and The Bottom Line

Michael Gerber is a genius. Every successful business person I meet has read Michael Gerber, refers to Michael Gerber, and lives by his words. You just can't get enough of Michael Gerber. He has the innate (and rare) ability to tap into one's soul, look deeply, and tell you what you need to hear. And then, he inspires you, equips you with the tools to get it done.

Pauline O'Malley, CEO, TheRevenueBuilder

When asked "Who was the most influential person in your life?" I am one of the thousands who don't hesitate to say "Michael E. Gerber." Michael helped transform me from someone dreaming of retirement to someone dreaming of working until age one hundred. This awakening is the predictable outcome of anyone reading Michael's new book.

Thomas O. Bardeen

Michael Gerber is an incredible business philosopher, guru, perhaps even a seer. He has an amazing intuition, which allows him to see in an instant what everybody else is missing; he sees opportunity everywhere. While in the Dreaming Room, Michael gave me the gift of seeing through the eyes of an awakened entrepreneur, and instantly my business changed from a regional success to serving clients on four continents.

Keith G. Schiehl, president, Rent-a-Geek Computer Services

Michael Gerber is among the very few who truly understand entrepreneurship and small business. While others talk about these topics in the form of theories, methodologies, processes, and so on, Michael goes to the heart of the issues. **Whenever Michael writes about entrepreneurship, soak it in as it is not only good for your business, but great for your soul.** His words will help you to keep your passion and balance while sailing through the uncertain sea of entrepreneurship.

Raymond Yeh, co-author, *The Art of Business*

Michael Gerber forced me to think big, think real, and gave me the support network to make it happen. A new wave of entrepreneurs is rising, much in thanks to his amazing efforts and very practical approach to doing business.

Christian Kessner, founder, Higher Ground Retreats and Events

Michael's understanding of entrepreneurship and small business management has been a difference maker for countless businesses, including Infusion Software. **His insights into the entrepreneurial process of building a business are a must-read for every small business owner.** The vision, clarity, and leadership that came out of our Dreaming Room experience were just what our company needed to recognize our potential and motivate the whole company to achieve it.

Clate Mask, president and CEO, Infusion Software

Michael Gerber is a truly remarkable man. His steady openness of mind and ability to get to the deeper level continues to be an inspiration and encouragement to me. **He seems to always ask that one question that forces the new perspective to break open and he approaches the new coming method in a fearless way.**

Rabbi Levi Cunin, Chabad of Malibu

The Dreaming Room experience was literally life-changing for us. **Within months, we were able to start our foundation and make several television appearances owing to his teachings.** He has an incredible charisma, which is priceless, but above all Michael Gerber *awakens* passion from within, enabling you to take action with dramatic results . . . starting today!

Shona and Shaun Carcary, Trinity Property Investments Inc.

—Home Vestors franchises

I thought *E-Myth* was an awkward name! What could this book do for me? **But when I finally got to reading it . . . it was what I was looking for all along.** Then, to top it off, I took a twenty-seven-hour trip to San Diego just to attend the Dreaming Room, where Michael touched my heart, my mind, and my soul.

Helmi Natto, president, Eye 2 Eye Optics, Saudi Arabia

I attended In the Dreaming Room and was challenged by Michael Gerber to "Go out and do what's impossible." So I did; **I became an author and international speaker and used Michael's principles to create a world-class company that will change and save lives all over the world.**

Dr. Don Kennedy, MBA; author, *5 AM & Already Behind*,

www.bahbits.com

The E Myth

Pest Control Business

Why Most Pest Control Businesses Don't Work and What to Do About It

MICHAEL E. GERBER
AUSTIN CLARK

PRODIGY
BUSINESS BOOKS

Published by
Prodigy Business Books, Inc., Carlsbad, California.

Production Team
Jordan S. Filkey, book production manager, The Tangible Nerd Co LLC;
Chris Groote, editor, Elk Mountain Concepts, LLC; Waqas Ali Dogar, cover
designer, Full Stop 360. Constantin Nimigean, book designer. Michael E. Gerber,
author and Austin Clark, co-author.

For general information on other products and services, please visit the website:
www.MichaelEGerberCompanies.com.

ISBN: 978-1-61835-004-6 (cloth)
ISBN: 978-1-61835-005-3 (audio)
ISBN: 978-1-61835-009-1 (ebook)

10 9 8 7 6 5 4 3 2 1

To Luz Delia Gerber, my partner, my wife, my inspiration, and my life ...Thank you for your perseverance, your indomitable will, and your kind and generous soul . . . You're spectacular!

—Michael E. Gerber

CONTENTS

A WORD ABOUT THIS BOOK

Michael E. Gerber

My first E-Myth book was published in 1985. It was the beginning of a long and enthralling exercise, called, by me, waking everyone up!

I named it, *The E-Myth: Why Most Businesses Don't Work and What to Do About It.*

The term, *E-Myth*, stood for the entrepreneurial myth. The fact that most small business owners aren't truly the entrepreneurs everyone thinks they are, but what I came to call, "technicians suffering from an entrepreneurial seizure!"

Since that book, and the company I created to provide business development services to its many readers, millions have read *The E-Myth* and the books that followed it, starting out with *The E-Myth Revisited*, and continuing with the more than 30 books which followed on its heels, along with the tens upon tens of thousands of small business owners who have participated in our E-Myth Mastery programs.

Since *The E-Myth Revisited* took the marketplace by storm, it became obvious to me that there was needed another series of books which addressed the application of my E-Myth Protocol in an entire subset of small companies, each of whom have been attracted to *The E-Myth* and applied its thinking to the extreme development of their uniquely designed Practices. The Practice of Law, or Chiropractic, of Landscape Contracting, et al. There are now eighteen of those "vertical books" addressing the seemingly unique problems of every field of endeavor, only to discover that my *E-Myth* Protocol has been applied successfully, and systematically, to each and every one of them.

So, my co-authors have become the most avid fans of our work, having told the story of how it has worked to grow their companies to a degree never thought possible before.

That's when the idea for this book series came about. What I think of as the Core Operating Series, co-authored by experts in each of the most critical strategic functions needing to be filled in every small growing company.

I think of those Strategic Functions as Financial, Legal, Operational, Strategic Leadership, Marketing, Technological, Social, and Administrative.

Think CFO, CEO, COO, CIO, CTO, CMO, CLO, and CAO.

In short, think getting one's house in order across the broad expanse of the Strategic Reach of any company as it grows from tiny to transformational.

It is our position that to be inordinately successful, every small company owner needs to assume the responsibility for each of these Eight Strategic Roles, until such time as he or she is able to replace him or herself with the individuals designated to fill those roles.

Since there's no better way of accomplishing an objective than by simply getting started with it, let's get started.

Allow me to introduce you to Austin Clark, a brilliant entrepreneur, who is committed to E-Myth Systems and creating profitable pest control businesses.

Welcome to *The E-Myth Pest Control Business!*

What a brilliant opportunity for each of us to grow exponentially and to understand how that works.

—Michael E. Gerber
Co-Founder, Chairman
Michael E. Gerber Companies, Inc.
Carlsbad, California
TheEmythPestControlBusiness.com

A NOTE FROM AUSTIN

When I first meet people, as we're making small talk about families and homes and careers, most are surprised that I'm in the pest control industry. They're even more surprised when I indicate that I'm part of a national brand.

As one shocked father told me at my son's game, "Austin, you don't look like *our* bug guy."

I guess that's true. I don't do field work. I have, and I still could, but fortunately, I learned rather quickly that field work, administration, and even office management wasn't really attractive to me.

Yet I've helped create the systems and processes to run a multi-million-dollar pest control company that has grown exponentially in the last decade.

To tell the truth though, it didn't start out like that. Pest Control, for me in the beginning, was simply a means to an end. I began working in the business as a salesperson, a college kid looking to make extra money to finance his mission trip. Now, two decades later, I'm an owner, and the systems I've helped to build have made us one of the fastest growing pest control companies in the United States.

We'll buy several million dollars' worth of smaller pest control businesses this year, just like we did last year, and we'll also grow in our home markets – usually in double digits, and often in the triple digits.

Why? A lot of reasons, but the biggest one is the reason you picked up this book: you're tired of the way your pest control business is running you. You're tired of being the only one who gets the work done. The only one who cares. The only one who gives a hoot.

You're tired of the endless cycle of sell and service, chasing down late payments, trying to hire people who can do the job, worrying about how to pay for all of this, worrying about how you'll somehow still be able to be a parent, or a spouse, or a friend, while you work sixty, or seventy, or eighty hours a week.

…And even after that, you're tired of wondering how you could have worked so hard and still have precious little to show for it.

"Where the heck is the money?" you might think, especially after you've been so "busy, busy, busy" all week, or all month, or all year.

Just like you did last year, and the year before that, and just like you'll do again this year when your accountant calls you to tell you how much you owe the IRS, or when the bookkeeper calls you at 4:55 on a Friday to tell you the payroll account doesn't have enough in it to cover this period's payroll, and what should she do about it?

I didn't write this book to beat my chest and tell you how much better I am than so many other hardworking men and women who have built successful pest control companies.

Not – At – All!

Frankly, I wrote it because I get frustrated seeing good people working their fingers to the bone in an industry I love. Especially when, with just a few changes, so many pest control companies and their owners could be so much more profitable.

They could be creating a legacy.

They could be enjoying their families, and their hobbies, and their lives.

I wrote it because I hoped that sharing what we've done at Moxie Pest Control of Arizona, headquartered in Phoenix, could help change the lives of thousands of people who have a pest control company that isn't giving them what they want.

So, as you stand there reading this and wondering, "Is this the book for me?", let me tell what you won't find in these pages...

You're not going to learn how to do your job faster.

I'm not going to make you more efficient ... at least not in the way you think of it right now.

There are few, if any, "hacks" in this book.

Nothing Michael and I are going to share in these pages is "easy."

Sounds a little disappointing, doesn't it?

Don't be. Here's what you will find, should you choose to keep reading...

How to reimagine your pest control business so you aren't the most necessary person in it.

A logical strategy to grow your company as large as you'd like, without your constant attention and management.

A business model based on Michael's teaching and studies of how to create a small business that actually works, alongside my own experience of doing just that in our industry.

The reality of our business – pest control – is that you, as an owner, should be focusing less on the skills and actions that make you better at the technical aspects of the job. Instead, the time has come for you to embrace a new way of thinking – one that allows you to continue to grow as an owner, and more importantly, as an entrepreneur.

If you're ready to do that, keep reading...

— Austin Clark
Moxie Pest Control of Arizona
Phoenix, Arizona

PREFACE

Michael E. Gerber

Over the past four decades, it's been my delight to inspire small business owners in every trade and profession to acquire and apply the methods and skills we've invented and perfected for the purpose of growing and thriving in their role as entrepreneur.

Most important in our work has been the Dream, Vision, Purpose and Mission that resides at the heart of it, without which nothing we've accomplished for the millions of small business owners we've reached out to and touched would have, could have, made any difference.

So too has that unadulterated passion been the source for our new, online business school, Radical U, whose purpose it is to transform the state of entrepreneurship and small business development in a manner never achieved or ever attempted, now available worldwide.

As you, a pest control business owner, read Austin Clark's story, and the absolutely profound success he's created utilizing my E-Myth Philosophy, Paradigm and tools, know that at the foundation of it all is the entrepreneurial energy and imagination now available to you all at Radical U™.

Austin and I invite you to join us there now by simply going to www.TheEmythPestControlBusiness.com

Welcome to the extraordinary world of INSPIRATION.

Welcome to the first day of the rest of your life!

Michael E. Gerber
Chief Dreamer
Co-Founder/Chairman
Michael E. Gerber Companies
Radical U™
Prodigy Business Books
The Dreaming Room™

ACKNOWLEDGMENTS

Michael E. Gerber

As always, and never to be forgotten, there are those who give of themselves to make my work possible.

To my dearest and most forgiving partner, wife, friend, and co-founder, Luz Delia Gerber, whose love and commitment takes me to places I would often not go unaccompanied.

To Chris Groote, noble warrior, editor, brave soul, and sojourner, who covers all the bases we would have missed had he not been there. To Constantine Nimigean, our stand-alone book designer, and Waqas Ali Dogar, who designed this cover - our visual geniuses who supported the creation of all things visual in this book we thank you, deeply, for your contributions. And to Jordan S. Filkey, whose work has been essential for you who are reading this.

To those many, many dreamers, thinkers, storytellers, and leaders, whose travels with me in The Dreaming Room have given me life, breath, and pleasure unanticipated before we met. To those many participants in my life (you know who you are), thank you for taking me seriously, and joining me in this exhilarating quest.

And, of course, to my co-authors, all of you, your genius, wisdom, intelligence, and wit have supplied me with a grand view of the world, which would never have been the same without you.

Love to all.

ACKNOWLEDGMENTS

Austin Clark

If there's one lesson that I hope this book teaches you about your own pest control business, it's this: *no man is an island.* The success each of us has is, to a large degree, based on the support, love, guidance, and actions of dozens (or even thousands) of other people.

In my own life, I cannot even begin to name them all, but there are those who come immediately to mind when I think about the journey that has brought me to this point in my life.

At the top of the list, of course, I have to place my wife, Ashtyn Clark, who has been not only a partner in this life, but done the seemingly impossible work of keeping so many things sorted in our family and life and allowing me the opportunity to learn what it means to be an entrepreneur.

To my parents, Brian and Delight Clark, who raised me to not only know the value of hard work, but also, the far more important values that make us better people: those of integrity, common sense, honesty, loyalty, and compassion.

As you'll soon learn in this book, no business exists in a vacuum, and there are countless men and women who have helped to boost ours. My business partner, Jason Walton, is at the top of that list. Over the years, he's proven to be the most trusting of people, quick to share and expand on opportunities we identified. At the same time, he's also been a valuable mentor to me, turning my own mistakes into teaching opportunities that made me a far better person and entrepreneur.

In that same light, I have to acknowledge our employees – past, present, and future. They have been open to change, they have been open to feedback, and they have allowed us to grow far beyond what we could ever have dreamed possible. Critically, they have afforded me the chance to step outside of the "busy-ness" to truly concentrate on the "business" and build a company worthy of their time.

The same can be said for our customers – they've shared what they expect, they've responded to the good (and the bad), and through it all, they've continued to support us and been open to the changes we've made as a company to better serve them.

…And this list, really, is far to short to acknowledge even a fraction of the people who have helped to create the entrepreneur I have become, and to all those unnamed – the mentors, the teachers, the friends, the teams, and the inspirations – you know the impact you've had on me and the business, and I thank you.

Lastly, to Michael – I sincerely appreciate the guidance you've provided to generations of entrepreneurs and the legacy you've given the world of small business.

INTRODUCTION

Michael E. Gerber

A s I write this book, the marketplace continues to do what it has always done; it goes up and it goes down. Today, in 2022, it's feverishly bearish.

Tomorrow, truly, the bottom could fall right out.

What has always been true, however, is that the marketplace lives by rules great companies don't.

The marketplace is an emotional storm, where rules one day defy attitudes the very next.

Where the truth on Monday is beset upon by a new truth like a ferocious dog on Tuesday.

If one were to run a company like the marketplace runs, disaster would be the common experience.

Come to think of it, while great companies do exactly the opposite of what the marketplace does, most companies unfortunately aren't great companies.

And that's why the vast majority of small companies which start up in any one year almost equal the number of small companies which close their doors in those very same years.

Think about it: for every one hundred new companies started, half of them fail in that very same year!

Doesn't matter what kind of company it is, either.

When a company, small or large, is operated based upon emotional decisions, that company is doomed to fail. And, from the very beginning to the very end, the vast majority of small companies are purely operated by emotional decisions, choices, preferences, opinions, attitudes, beliefs, and hopes.

Thus, this book.

The Story of Steve and Peggy

Michael E. Gerber

Make every detail perfect, and limit the number of details to perfect.
—Jack Dorsey, founder of Twitter

E very business is a family business. To ignore this truth is to court disaster.

I don't care if family members actually work in the business or not. Whatever his or her relationship with the business, every member of a pest control business owner's family will be greatly affected by the decisions the owner makes about the business. There's just no way around it.

Unfortunately, like most business owners, pest control contractors tend to compartmentalize their lives. They view their trade as a profession—what they do—and therefore none of their family's business.

"This has nothing to do with you," says the owner to his wife, with blind conviction. "I leave work at the office and family at home."

And with equal conviction, I say, "Not true!"

In actuality, your family and your pest control business are inextricably linked to one another. What's happening in your business is also happening at home. Consider the following and ask yourself if each is true:

- If you're angry at work, you're also angry at home.
- If you're out of control in your business, you're equally out of control at home.
- If you're having trouble with money in your company, you're also having trouble with money at home.
- If you have communication problems in your business, you're also having communication problems at home.
- If you don't trust in your company, you don't trust at home.
- If you're secretive in your business, you're equally secretive at home.

And you're paying a huge price for it!

The truth is that your business and your family are one—and you're the link. Or you should be. Because if you try to keep your business and your family apart, if your business and your family are strangers, you will effectively create two separate worlds that can never wholeheartedly serve each other. Two worlds that split each other apart.

Let me tell you the story of Steve and Peggy Walsh.

The Walshes met while in college. They were lab partners in their sophomore biology class, Steve a biology student and Peggy a business management student. When their lab discussions started to wander beyond Punnett Squares into their personal lives, they discovered they had a lot in common. By the end of the course, they weren't just talking in class; they were talking on the phone every night … and *not* about their latest lab homework.

Steve thought Peggy was absolutely brilliant (her love for dogs was astounding), and Peggy considered Steve the most passionate man she knew. It wasn't long before they were engaged and planning their future together. A week after graduation, they were married in a lovely garden ceremony in Peggy's childhood home.

While Steve was able to apply his degree and personality with a local pest control company, Peggy landed an administrative position with a large landscaping contractor in the city. Over the next few years, the couple worked hard to keep their finances afloat. They worked long hours, and the end of each day found them exhausted, and despite Peggy's thriftiness with money, the young couple still struggled to make ends meet. But throughout it all, they were committed to what they were doing and to each other.

After Steve had received all the proper certifications from the NPMA, he was able to use his experience to secure a more lucrative position with a national pest control company at a significantly higher salary while Peggy began working at a large landscape contracting company nearby. Soon afterward, the couple had their first son, and Peggy decided to take some time off from her career to be with him. Those were good years. Steve and Peggy loved each other very much, were active members in their church, participated in community organizations, and spent quality time together. The Walshes considered themselves one of the most fortunate families they knew.

But work became troublesome. Steve grew increasingly frustrated with the way the company was run. "I want to go into business for myself," he announced one night at the dinner table. "I want to start my own company."

Steve and Peggy spent many nights talking about the move. Was it something they could afford? Did Steve really have the skills necessary to make a pest control business a success? Were there enough customers to go around? What impact would such a move have on Peggy's own career when she went back to work, their lifestyle, their son, their relationship? They asked all the questions they thought they needed to answer before Steve went into business for himself ... but they never really drew up a concrete plan.

Finally, tired of talking and confident that he could handle whatever he might face, Steve committed to starting his own pest control company. Because she loved and supported him, Peggy agreed, offering her own commitment to help in any way she could.

So Steve quit his job, took out a second mortgage on their home, and leased a small office in an industrial complex nearby.

In the beginning, things went well. A housing boom had hit the town, and new families were pouring into the area. Steve had no trouble getting new customers. His business expanded, quickly outgrowing his office.

Within a year, Steve had employed an office manager, Clarissa, to book appointments and handle the administrative side of the business. He also hired a bookkeeper, Tim, to handle the finances. Steve was ecstatic with the progress his young business had made. He celebrated by taking his wife and son on vacation to Italy.

Of course, managing a business was more complicated and time-consuming than working for someone else. Steve not only supervised all the jobs Clarissa and Tim did, he was continually looking for work to keep everyone busy. When he wasn't scanning trade journals to stay abreast of what was going on in the field or fulfilling continuing-education requirements to stay current on his certifications, he was going to the bank, wading through customer paperwork, or speaking with vendors (which usually degenerated into *arguing* with vendors). He also found himself spending more and more time on the telephone dealing with customer complaints and nurturing relationships.

As the months went by and more and more customers came through the door, Steve had to spend even more time just trying to keep his head above water.

By the end of its second year, the company, now employing two full-time and two part-time people, had moved to a larger office downtown. The demands on Steve's time had grown with the company.

He began leaving home earlier in the morning, returning home later at night. He drank more. He rarely saw his son anymore. For the most part, Steve was resigned to the problem. He saw the hard work as essential to building the "sweat equity" he had long heard about.

Money was also becoming a problem for Steve. Although the business was growing like crazy, money always seemed scarce when it was really needed.

When Steve had worked for somebody else, he had been paid twice a month. In his own business, he often had to wait— sometimes for months. He was still owed money on billings he had completed more than ninety days before.

Of course, no matter how slowly Steve got paid, he still had to pay *his* people. This became a relentless problem. Steve often felt like a juggler dancing on a tightrope. A fire burned in his stomach day and night.

To make matters worse, Steve began to feel that Peggy was insensitive to his troubles. Not that he often talked to his wife about the company. "Business is business" was Steve's mantra. "It's my responsibility to handle things at the office and Peggy's responsibility to take care of her own job and the family."

Peggy herself was working weekend hours at the landscape company, and they'd brought in a nanny to help with their son. Steve couldn't help but notice that his wife seemed resentful, and her apparent lack of understanding baffled him. Didn't she see that he had a company to take care of? That he was doing it all for his family? Apparently not.

As time went on, Steve became even more consumed and frustrated by his business. When he went off on his own, he remembered saying, "I don't like people telling me what to do." But people were *still* telling him what to do.

Not surprisingly, Peggy grew more frustrated by her husband's lack of communication. She cut back on her own hours to focus on their family, but her husband still never seemed to be around. Their relationship grew tense and strained. The rare moments they *were* together were more often than not peppered by long silences—a far cry from the heartfelt conversations that had characterized their relationship's early days, when they'd talk into the wee hours of the morning.

Meanwhile, Tim, the bookkeeper, was also becoming a problem for Steve. Tim never seemed to have the financial information Steve needed to make decisions about payroll, customer billing, and general operating expenses, let alone how much money was available for Steve and Peggy's living expenses.

When questioned, Tim would shift his gaze to his feet and say, "Listen, Steve, I've got a lot more to do around here than you can imagine. It'll take a little more time. Just don't press me, okay?"

Overwhelmed by his own work, Steve usually backed off. The last thing Steve wanted was to upset Tim and have to do the books himself. He could also empathize with what Tim was going through, given the business's growth over the past year.

Late at night in his office, Steve would sometimes recall his first years out of school. He missed the simple life he and his family had shared. Then, as quickly as the thoughts came, they would vanish. He had work to do and no time for daydreaming. "Having my own company is a great thing," he would remind himself. "I simply have to apply myself, as I did in school, and get on with the job. I have to work as hard as I always have when something needed to get done."

Steve began to live most of his life inside his head. He began to distrust his people. They never seemed to work hard enough or to care about his company as much as he did. If he wanted to get something done, he usually had to do it himself.

Then one day, the office manager, Clarissa, quit in a huff, frustrated by the amount of work that her boss was demanding of her. Steve was left with a desk full of papers and a telephone that wouldn't stop ringing.

Clueless about the work Clarissa had done, Steve was overwhelmed by having to pick up the pieces of a job he didn't understand. His world turned upside down. He felt like a stranger in his own company.

Why had he been such a fool? Why hadn't he taken the time to learn what Clarissa did in the office? Why had he waited until now?

Ever the trouper, Steve plowed into Clarissa's job with everything he could muster. What he found shocked him. Clarissa's workspace was a disaster area! Her desk drawers were a jumble of papers, coins, pens, pencils, rubber bands, envelopes, business cards, contact lenses, eye drops, and candy.

"What was she thinking?" Steve raged.

When he got home that night, even later than usual, he got into a shouting match with Peggy. He settled it by storming out of the house to get a drink. Didn't anybody understand him? Didn't anybody care what he was going through?

He returned home only when he was sure Peggy was asleep. He slept on the couch and left early in the morning, before anyone was awake. He was in no mood for questions or arguments.

When Steve got to his office the next morning, he immediately headed for the makeshift kitchen, nervously looking for some Tylenol to get rid of his throbbing headache.

What lessons can we draw from Steve and Peggy's story? I've said it once and I'll say it again: *Every business is a family business.* Your business profoundly touches every member of your family, even if they never set foot inside your office. Every business either gives to the family or takes from the family, just as individual family members do.

If the business takes more than it gives, the family is always the first to pay the price.

In order for Steve to free himself from the prison he created, he would first have to admit his vulnerability. He would have to confess to himself and his family that he really didn't know enough about his own business and how to grow it.

Steve tried to do it all himself. Had he succeeded, had the company supported his family in the style he imagined, he would have burst with pride. Instead, Steve unwittingly isolated himself, thereby achieving the exact opposite of what he sought.

He destroyed his life—and his family's life along with it.

Repeat after me: Every business is a family business.

Are you like Steve? I believe that all business owners share a common soul with him. You must learn that a business is only a business. It is not your life. But it is also true that your business can have a profoundly negative impact on your life unless you learn how to do it differently than most contractors do it—and definitely differently than Steve did it.

Steve's pest control business could have served his and his family's life. But for that to happen, he would have had to learn how to master his business in a way that was completely foreign to him.

Instead, Steve's business consumed him. Because he lacked a true understanding of the essential strategic thinking that would have allowed him to create something unique, Steve and his family were doomed from day one.

This book contains the secrets that Steve should have known. If you follow in Steve's footsteps, prepare to have your life and business fall apart. But if you apply the principles we'll discuss here, you can avoid a similar fate.

Let's start with the subject of *money*. But, before we do, let's read a pest control contractor's view about the story I just told you. Let's talk about Austin's journey . . . and yours. ✤

The Story of Austin and Ashtyn

Austin Clark

"Everyone needs a house to live in, but a supportive family is what builds a home."

– Anthony Liccione

No story can ever be told completely, but this story cannot be told at all without two things: my wife, Ashtyn, and my life in the pest control business. And while it might feel strange to bring my professional life into my personal life, or vice versa, as Michael has said, *every* business is a family business.

…And so it is – and was – with us.

The earliest days of my career were also the earliest days of my marriage.

The goals we set as a couple coincided with goals I had set for myself as – in those days, a young man selling pest control services door to door.

Even the plans we made for us – in terms of the summers between semesters – revolved around our relationship and where my role in the company required me to be. Dallas, Phoenix,

Oklahoma City. Wherever I was needed simply meant my family would be there, too.

As time passed, and our first son was born, even a growing family and growing business opportunities posed no threat to my career, and that same career posed no threat to my family. Growth begat growth.

I'm not telling you this because I had it all figured out; not at all. In fact, when I think back to those earliest years of my marriage and the business I would one day own, I'm shocked at the results!

In many ways it was no different than the story that could be told by thousands of other men and women in the pest control industry.

I found myself "busy, busy, busy" and "doin' it, doin' it, doin' it" day after day, week after week, and the results of that hard work seemed to be paying off. Our small business was growing, and I believed people when they told me that we'd have to go through growing pains.

But after all these years, I think I understand a little more about life, and marriage, and building a business, and it comes down to one thing: *a family that's a team.* Ashtyn was – and is – the rock I could build everything from and with. She understood when work took me away late at night, or out of town for weeks at a time. She didn't follow with blind faith, she didn't just quietly accept any excuse or reason, but she supported the decisions I made, and I supported the decisions she made.

Now, I'm not qualified to give you relationship advice, but I can look back on the growth and success we've created as a company and honestly tell you – it came because I felt supported. I had the relative luxury of knowing my wife was equally as passionate about my success as I was. More importantly, I never once felt alone.

Silencing the Noise

Let's face it, being an entrepreneur can be lonely. Who do you talk to? Your employees have employee problems, other business owners are sure you've somehow got things better than they do, and even your oldest friends can only empathize with you because they don't truly understand what entrepreneurship looks like. Your problems and your victories come home with you, and you'll either have someone to share them with or you'll have to sit and stew in them.

The reality is I'm not any smarter than anyone else, but when we started this journey, I knew that a marriage and a business could not grow and succeed if everyone is just doing the same thing.

We've all seen the construction on roads and highways, and wondered at how anything can possibly get done. It always seems as though one person is working while a half a dozen others watch. As the taxpayers footing that bill, we can be frustrated by how little "work" seems to be happening, and yet, in the end, that road, or bridge, or viaduct is completed. I see the same thing happening in marriages and businesses.

One person, unsure of what their business partner or spouse is doing - maybe they'll say something, maybe they won't. But sooner or later? It WILL be brought up. The results are usually the same – angry words, bitterness, and – in some cases – a failed partnership.

I never once felt that with Ashtyn, and I can tell you why: We talked. We made plans. We stayed organized. Do you do that now with the people you live with and love and know better than anyone else in the world?

Do you share your dream, your vision, your purpose, and your mission with them?

Have you told the men and women you've partnered with in business?

I'm willing to bet you haven't, and it's affecting your company and your home.

So, the very first thing, the first tentative steps to attaining the success you want to have HAS to be this: you're a fool to do it alone. You're also incredibly selfish if you refuse to share your goals (and your worries) at home. Ashtyn heard everything – and still does – and you know what?

She listened. She supported me. She kicked my butt when I needed it.

Did she worry? Have doubts? Wonder how we'd ever make it as big as we have? I'm sure she did, but she kept her counsel and instead of choosing to break me down in a moment of weakness, she offered hope. Ideas. A safe place for our dreams to grow.

You've got to have that too, especially if, like so many pest control owners, you *are* the company.

In the last chapter, when Michael shared the Story of Steve and Peggy, how many times did you find yourself nodding your head? When I read that, and many times when I talk to other people who own pest control companies, I hear stories that sound exactly like that. Angry words at home, discord among partners, and a veritable avalanche of bad decisions that lead to closed doors, failed businesses, and ended marriages.

Let me tell you right now, before you read another page, you can't hide your business from your family, and you can't hide your family from your business. Now, your spouse absolutely can play a role in the business – if they want to.

But it's not required.

You need to know the level of commitment they have so you can understand their level of passion. You can't be angry if your spouse is working in your pest control business answering phones, handling dispatch duties and acting like an employee.

That's what you've asked them to be!

As I look back on what we've done to help create this business and the steps we've taken, I know that Ashtyn would happily step up to do anything she could, but, for me at least, the real beauty of the role she's played in our success as a company was simple: she believed in me, sometimes more than I believed in myself.

The Real Test

Until you test something, you can never know it's true strength. That holds true for the systems in businesses, fail safes in a computer program, or a marriage. In 2013, I'm NOT pleased to say, my focus on growth within Moxie led to one of the biggest tests of my own marriage.

Remember when I said I have always felt supported by Ashtyn?

As a result of the hyper growth we were experiencing in the company, one day I found myself short nearly $8,000 to make payroll. Cash was rolling in – and rolling right back out – but the actual funds we needed to make payroll simply weren't there.

I couldn't take out another loan.

My credit, both personal and professional, was tapped out.

I was desperate to find the money to pay my people and – in reality – everything we had worked so hard to build. I had to take Ashtyn's car to a title loan company. In exchange for the title to her car, I got the money I needed to make payroll.

Now you might not know how that system works, but basically, I had to give the loan company the title to Ashtyn's car in exchange for the money I needed, paying them back at an incredibly high interest rate for the loan, or they'd take the car.

You can imagine how embarrassing that was, and far worse? It wasn't my car, but Ashtyn's.

Talk about motivation to get my business finances in order!

My point in telling you this story is this: how would your spouse feel if you did this?

Have you created the relationship with them – by sharing your passion and your plans – so they would still support you if you'd screwed up this badly? I'm not suggesting that they'd blindly accept it – my wife most certainly was upset – but she knew in her heart that I was embarrassed and ashamed.

She could have beat me up over it, but she chose not to.

She could have thrown in the towel, but she chose not to.

Instead, she asked me to fix the problem I'd created; to rethink the processes that had led us to that moment.

Her support meant more than anything else, and guess what?

It changed everything for me and for my focus in the business.

I dug into cashflow, I dug into income, and profits, and peculiar problems that "money" can create.

…And gradually, over time, the needle moved. Month after month and year after year.

Why? Simple. I had someone in my corner. Ashtyn. She's still there, and she still inspires me, and as much as the story of Moxie is the story of growth and systems and processes and hard work, it's also the story of a woman who believed in her husband, even when he pawned her car. ✤

CHAPTER

3

On the Subject
of Money

Michael E. Gerber

If money is your hope for independence, you will never have it. The only real security that a man will have in this world is a reserve of knowledge, experience, and ability.

—Henry Ford

Had Steve and Peggy first considered the subject of *money* as we will here, their lives could have been radically different. Money is on the tip of every business owner's tongue, on the edge (or at the very center) of every contractor's thoughts, intruding on every part of a contractor's life.

With money consuming so much energy, why do so few pest control business owners handle it well? Why was Steve, like so many others, willing to entrust his financial affairs to a relative stranger? Why is money scarce for most business owners? Why is there less money than expected? And yet the demand for money is *always* greater than anticipated.

What is it about money that is so elusive, so complicated, so difficult to control? Why is it that every contractor I've ever met hates to deal with the subject of money? Why are they almost always too late in facing money problems? And why are they constantly obsessed with the desire for more of it?

Money—you can't live with it and you can't live without it. But you'd better understand it and get your people to understand it. Because until you do, money problems will eat your business for lunch.

You don't need an accountant or financial planner to do this. You simply need to prod your people to relate to money very personally. From technician to receptionist, they should all understand the financial impact of what they do every day in relationship to the profit and loss of the company.

And so you must teach your people to think like owners, not like technicians or office managers or receptionists. You must teach them to operate like personal profit centers, with a sense of how their work fits in with the company as a whole.

You must involve everyone in the business with the topic of money—how it works, where it goes, how much is left, and how much everybody gets at the end of the day. You also must teach them about the four kinds of money created by the business.

The Four Kinds of Money

In the context of owning, operating, developing, and exiting from a pest control business, money can be split into four distinct but highly integrated categories:

- Income
- Profit
- Flow
- Equity

Failure to distinguish how the four kinds of money play out in your business is a surefire recipe for disaster.

Important note: Do *not* talk to your accountants or bookkeepers about what follows; it will only confuse you. The information comes from the real-life experiences of thousands of small business owners, pest control owners included, most of whom were hopelessly confused about money when I met them. Once they understood and accepted the following principles, they developed a clarity about money that could only be called enlightened.

The First Kind of Money: Income

Income is the money a company pays its employees for doing their job *in* the business, including the pest control contractor/owner. It's what they get paid for going to work every day.

Clearly, if pest control contractors didn't do their job, others would have to, and *they* would be paid the money the business currently pays the contractors. Income, then, has nothing to do with *ownership*. Income is solely the province of *employeeship*.

That's why to the pest control technician-as-*employee*, Income is the most important form money can take. To the pest control contractor-as-*owner*, however, it is the *least* important form money can take.

Most important; least important. Do you see the conflict? The conflict between the technician-as-employee and the contractor-as-owner?

We'll deal with this conflict later. For now, just know that it is potentially the most paralyzing conflict in a contractor's life.

Failing to resolve this conflict will cripple you. Resolving it will set you free.

The Second Kind of Money: Profit

Profit is what's left over after a pest control contractor's business has done its job effectively and efficiently. If there is no profit, the business is doing something wrong.

However, just because the business shows a profit does not mean it is necessarily doing all the right things in the right way. Instead, it just means that something was done right during or preceding the period in which the profit was earned.

The important issue here is whether the profit was intentional or accidental. If it happened by accident (which most profit does), don't take credit for it. You'll live to regret your impertinence.

If it happened intentionally, take all the credit you want. You've earned it. Because profit created intentionally, rather than by accident, is replicable—again and again. And your business's ability to repeat its performance is the most critical ability it can have.

As you'll soon see, the value of money is a function of your business's ability to produce it in predictable amounts at an above-average return on investment.

Profit can be understood only in the context of your business purpose, as opposed to *your* purpose as a pest control contractor. Profit, then, fuels the forward motion of the business that produces it. This is accomplished in four ways:

- Profit is *investment capital* that feeds and supports growth.
- Profit is *bonus capital* that rewards people for exceptional work.
- Profit is *operating capital* that shores up money shortfalls.
- Profit is *return-on-investment* capital that rewards you, the contractor-owner, for taking risks.

Without profit, a pest control business cannot subsist, much less grow. Profit is the fuel of progress.

If a business misuses or abuses profit, however, the penalty is much like having no profit at all. Imagine the plight of a pest control contractor who has way too much return-on-investment capital and not enough investment capital, bonus capital, and operating capital. Can you see the imbalance this creates?

The Third Kind of Money: Flow

Flow is what money *does* in a pest control business, as opposed to what money *is*. Whether the business is large or small, money tends to move erratically through it, much like a pinball. One minute it's there; the next minute it's not.

Flow can be even more critical to a business' survival than profit, because a business can produce a profit and still be short of money. Has this ever happened to you? It's called profit on paper rather than in fact.

No matter how large your business, if the money isn't there when it's needed, you're threatened—regardless of how much profit you've made. You can borrow it, of course. But money acquired in dire circumstances is almost always the most expensive kind of money you can get.

Knowing where the money is and where it will be when you need it is a critically important task of both the technician-as-employee and the contractor-as-owner.

Rules of Flow

You will learn no lesson more important than the huge impact flow can have on the health and survival of your pest control sole proprietorship, let alone your business or enterprise. The following two rules will help you understand why this subject is so critical.

1. **The First Rule of Flow states that your income statement is static, while the flow is dynamic.** Your income statement is a snapshot, while the flow is a moving picture. So, while your income statement is an excellent tool for analyzing your

business *after* the fact, it's a poor tool for managing it in the heat of the moment.

Your income statement tells you (1) how much money you're spending and where, and (2) how much money you're receiving and from where.

Flow gives you the same information as the income statement, plus it tells you *when* you're spending and receiving money. In other words, flow is an income statement moving through time. And that is the key to understanding flow. It is about management in real time. How much is coming in? How much is going out? You'd like to know this daily, or even by the hour if possible. Never by the week or month.

You must be able to forecast flow. You must have a flow plan that helps you gain a clear vision of the money that's out there next month and the month after that. You must also pinpoint what your needs will be in the future.

Ultimately, however, when it comes to flow, the action is always in the moment. It's about *now*. The minute you start to meander away from the present, you'll miss the boat.

Unfortunately, few pest control business owners pay any attention to flow until it dries up completely and slow pay becomes no pay. They are oblivious to this kind of detail until, say, customers announce that they won't pay for this or that. That gets a contractor's attention because the expenses keep on coming.

When it comes to flow, most pest control contractors are flying by the proverbial seat of their pants. No matter how many people you hire to take care of your money, until you change the way you think about it, you will always be out of luck. No one can do this for you.

Managing flow takes attention to detail. But when flow is managed, your life takes on an incredible sheen. You're swimming with the current, not against it. You're in charge!

2.   **The Second Rule of Flow states that money seldom moves as you expect it to.** But you do have the power to change that,

provided you understand the two primary sources of money as it comes in and goes out of your pest control business.

The truth is, the more control you have over the *source* of money, the more control you have over its flow. The sources of money are both inside and outside of your business.

Money comes from *outside* your business in the form of receivables, reimbursements, investments, and loans.

Money comes from *inside* your business in the form of payables, taxes, capital investments, and payroll. These are the costs associated with attracting customers, delivering your services, operations, and so forth.

Few contractors see the money going *out* of their business as a source of money, but it is.

When considering how to spend money in your business, you can save—and therefore make—money in three ways:

- Do it more effectively.
- Do it more efficiently.
- Stop doing it altogether.

By identifying the money sources inside and outside of your business, and then applying these methods, you will be immeasurably better at controlling the flow in your business.

But what are these sources? They include how you:

- manage your services;
- buy supplies and equipment;
- compensate your people;
- plan people's use of time;
- determine the direct cost of your services;
- increase the number of customers you see;
- manage your work;
- collect reimbursements and receivables

In fact, every task performed in your business (and ones you haven't yet learned how to perform) can be done more efficiently and effectively, dramatically reducing the cost of doing business. In the process, you will create more income, produce more profit, and balance the flow.

The Fourth Kind of Money: Equity

Sadly, few pest control contractors fully appreciate the value of equity in their pest control business. Yet equity is the second most valuable asset any contractor will ever possess. (The first most valuable asset is, of course, your life. More on that later.)

Equity is the financial value placed on your pest control business by a prospective buyer.

Thus, your *business* is your most important product, not your services. Because your business has the power to set you free. That's right. Once you sell your business—providing you get what you want for it—you're free!

Of course, to enhance your equity, to increase your business's value, you have to build it right. You have to build a business that works. A business that can become a true business, and a business that can become a true enterprise. A company/business/enterprise that can produce income, profit, flow, and equity better than any other pest control business can.

To accomplish that, your business must be designed so that it can do what it does systematically and predictably, every single time.

The Story of McDonald's

Let me tell you the most unlikely story anyone has ever told you about the successful building of a pest control company, business, and enterprise. Let me tell you the story of Ray Kroc.

You might be thinking, "What on earth does a hamburger stand have to do with my business? I'm not in the hamburger business; I'm a pest control contractor!"

Yes, you are. But by mitigating pests as you have been taught, you've abandoned any chance to expand your reach, help more customers, or improve your services the way they must be improved if the business of pest control—and your life—is going to be transformed.

In Ray Kroc's story lies the answer.

Kroc called his first McDonald's restaurant "a little money machine." That's why thousands of franchises bought it. And the reason it worked? Kroc demanded consistency, so that a hamburger in Philadelphia would be an advertisement for one in Peoria. In fact, no matter where you bought a McDonald's hamburger in the 1950s, the meat patty was guaranteed to weigh exactly 1.6 ounces, with a diameter of $3^5/_8$ inches. It was in the McDonald's Operations Manual.

Did Kroc succeed? You know he did! And so can you, once you understand his methods. Consider just one part of his story.

In 1954, Kroc made his living selling the five-spindle Multimixer milkshake machine. He heard about a hamburger stand in San Bernardino, California, that had eight of his machines in operation, meaning it could make forty shakes simultaneously. This he had to see.

Kroc flew from Chicago to Los Angeles, then drove sixty miles to San Bernardino. As he sat in his car outside Mac and Dick McDonald's restaurant, he watched as lunch customers lined up for bags of hamburgers.

In a revealing moment, Kroc approached a strawberry blonde in a yellow convertible. As he later described it, "It was not her sex appeal but the obvious relish with which she devoured the hamburger that made my pulse begin to hammer with excitement."

Passion.

In fact, it was the French fry that truly captured his heart. Before the 1950s, it was almost impossible to buy fries of consistent quality. Kroc changed all that. "The French fry," he once wrote, "would become almost sacrosanct for me, its preparation a ritual to be followed religiously."

Passion and preparation.

The potatoes had to be just so—top-quality Idaho russets, eight ounces apiece, deep-fried to a golden brown, and salted with a shaker that, as Kroc put it, kept going "like a Salvation Army girl's tambourine."

As Kroc soon learned, potatoes too high in water content—and even top-quality Idaho russets varied greatly in water content—will come out soggy when fried. And so Kroc sent out teams of workers, armed with hydrometers, to make sure all his suppliers were producing potatoes in the optimal solids range of 20 to 23 percent.

Preparation and passion. Passion and preparation. Look those words up in the dictionary and you'll see Kroc's picture. Can you envision your picture there?

Do you understand what Kroc did? Do you see why he was able to sell thousands of franchises? Kroc knew the true value of equity, and, unlike Steve from our story, Kroc went to work *on* his business rather than *in* his business. He knew the hamburger wasn't his product—McDonald's was!

So what does *your* pest control business need to do to become a little money machine? What is the passion that will drive you to build a business that works—a turnkey system like Ray Kroc's?

Equity and the Turnkey System

What's a turnkey system? And why is it so valuable to you? To better understand it, let's look at another example of a turnkey system that worked to perfection: the recordings of Frank Sinatra.

Sinatra's records were to him as McDonald's restaurants were to Ray Kroc. They were part of a turnkey system that allowed Sinatra to sing to millions of people without having to be there himself.

Sinatra's recordings were a dependable turnkey system that worked predictably, systematically, automatically, and effortlessly to produce the same results every single time—no matter where they were played, and no matter who was listening.

Regardless of where Sinatra was, his records just kept on producing income, profit, flow, and equity, over and over ... and still do! Sinatra needed only to produce the prototype recording and the system did the rest.

Kroc's McDonald's is another prototypical turnkey solution, addressing everything McDonald's needs to do in a basic, systematic way so that anyone properly trained by McDonald's can successfully reproduce the same results.

And this is where you'll realize your equity opportunity: in the way your company does business; in the way your business systematically does what you intend it to do; and in the development of your turnkey system—a system that works even in the hands of ordinary people (and pest control contractors less experienced than you) to produce extraordinary results.

Remember:

- If you want to build vast equity in your business, then go to work *on* your business, building it into a business that works every single time.
- Go to work *on* your business to build a totally integrated turnkey system that delivers exactly what you promised every single time.
- Go to work *on* your business to package it and make it stand out from the pest control businesses you see everywhere else.

Here is the most important idea you will ever hear about your business and what it can potentially provide for you:

The value of your equity is directly proportional to how well your business works. And how well your business works is directly proportional to the effectiveness of the systems you have put into place upon which the operation of your business depends.

Whether money takes the form of income, profit, flow, or equity, the amount of it—and how much of it stays with you—invariably boils down to this. Money, happiness, life—it all depends on how well your business works. Not on your people, not on you, but on the system.

Your business holds the secret to more money. Are you ready to learn how to find it?

Earlier in this chapter, I alerted you to the inevitable conflict between the technician-as-employee and the contractor-as-owner. It's a battle between the part of you working *in* the business and the part of you working *on* the business. Between the part of you working for income and the part of you working for equity.

Here's how to resolve this conflict:

1. Be honest with yourself about whether you're filling *employee* shoes or *owner* shoes.

2. As your business's key employee, determine the most effective way to do the job you're doing, *and then document that job.*

3. Once you've documented the job, create a strategy for replacing yourself with someone else (another technician, or, even better, a contractor) who will then use your documented system *exactly* as you do.

4. Have your new employees manage the newly delegated system. Improve the system by quantifying its effectiveness over time.

5. Repeat this process throughout your business wherever you catch yourself acting as employee rather than owner.

Learn to distinguish between ownership work and employee-ship work every step of the way.

Master these methods, understand the difference between the four kinds of money, develop an interest in how money works in your business … and then watch it flow in with the speed and efficiency of a variable capacity compressor.

Now let's take another step in our strategic thinking process. Let's look at the subject of *planning*. But first, let's see what Austin has to say about *money*. ❧

CHAPTER

4

Coming to Grips with the Money

Austin Clark

"If we command our wealth, we shall be rich and free; if our wealth commands us, we are poor indeed."

—Edmund Burke

L et's be honest, the reason we're in business is to make money. Yes, we can all use words like "freedom" and "flexibility" or "control" to validate our decision to own and operate a pest control company, but it really comes down to the decision we've made of the system we'd like to use to make money.

Don't worry – I'm not going to judge you for it because I made the same decision. On the other hand, in my experience there is a wide gap between how many pest control owners view and use money and the systemized solution Michael shared in the last chapter.

Why?

Simple: Most pest control owners act like technicians, not entrepreneurs.

Because of that, they're viewing their business income as their personal income.

...They don't understand the truth of "profit".

...Their concept of "flow" is all wrong.

...And the idea of "equity" is restricted to only the tools and equipment they own.

In other words, no matter how good these pest control owners can do the technical work of the business, they are allowing themselves to fail because they've never taken the next step to grow as entrepreneurs.

The good news is we can change that!

Fixing the Income Disconnect

To begin with, as an owner you have to understand there is a difference between Income and Profit. If you sell a home treatment for $250, the various chemicals might cost $10; the fuel you use to get you and your equipment there might be $20; and then, you might have some disposable PPE (personal protective equipment) that is $10.

So, the quick math tells us that $250 treatment yields us $210 after we pay for the materials.

An owner with a technician's mindset looks at that visit and sees $210 in profit.

An owner with an entrepreneur's mindset recognizes there are two more important steps: they need to be paid for their time and they need to allocate funds to pay for taxes. Now, what you choose to pay yourself or your technicians for the work done on a single call is up to you, but for every dollar that is paid to your company, you need to plan on 30+% being used for taxes.

Yes. Taxes. In this example ($250), let's use 30% as the tax rate, so $75. When we subtract that from the remaining $210, we've got $135 still "on the table." If we pay ourselves or our tech $50, that leaves a remaining profit of $85.

This is just a basic illustration! We haven't paid for our trucks, any financed equipment, our shop, and so on, but the point is, many owners of small pest control businesses can't (or won't) make this first critical distinction: Your income is not your profit, and your profit is not your income!

Right now, though, you might be thinking, "Austin, how did you come to own a huge business being so dumb! I hardly pay anything in taxes! My bookkeeper and accountant help me manage that waaaaay down. Just buy stuff for the business!"

This book isn't a book on taxes but let me take a moment to respond to the silly idea (and terrible advice) too many pest control business owners use to "manage their taxes."

The idea sounds good: you spend business profits to claim business deductions and credits and mitigate your tax bill. The $100,000 diesel truck you're driving for "business." The family trip you took last year where you attended one "meeting" at Disney and wrote the rest of the trip off as "business." The dinners you and your spouse go on every Friday and charge to the business since you talked about your company waiting on your cheese fries to be delivered.

Yes, all of those actions do lower your tax liabilities, but they eat up your business profits.

Here's why it's a bad idea: the profits your business generate (and thus, the taxes you pay) will be a deciding factor in your ability to create lines of credit for your company, to borrow money for your business, and to assign a real value to your company when it comes time to sell it. Don't hide from taxes, because you're really only hiding from profits!

One of the first actions I take, when reviewing a pest control business for a possible purchase, is to see what their annual profits are.

I can take five minutes to look at a company's top-line sales and their bottom line profits and learn far more than an owner would ever tell me.

Okay, rant over. Seriously, though, these first steps – understanding profits and taxes – are critical for you, as the owner, to allow a pest control company to actually grow beyond the job you created for yourself.

The E-Myth teaches us to build a system that can be taught and used by average people with average skills. Indeed, one need only look to Ray Kroc and McDonalds to see how well such a system can work. So, when it comes to your personal income when you do the work of a pest control technician, the numbers are easy to find, and thus one aspect of your own income is simple to understand.

But what about that company profit?

As I said, there's a lot more to it than what got used on a service call, and so from the E-Myth point of view, we need to understand the longer-term expenses – the trucks, the equipment, the shop, and so on. When those are paid each month, our earlier number - $85 per sales call – is actually much smaller. In fact, many times when I speak with pest control companies around the country, when we begin to analyze these "real" profit numbers, we find that some service calls cost their company money!

It's ALL in the Flow

The beauty of taking this type of action in your own company is you can easily see how and when growth can happen. What are the costs of bringing on new technicians? Buying new vehicles and equipment? Expanding your area of operations?

Even more importantly, you'll begin – maybe for the first time – to see the actual flow of money through your company.

Let me ask you, have you ever heard from your bookkeeper or CPA that your accounts are overdrawn, and you can't understand why?

More than likely it's because you've never stopped to look at your costs.

At your actions.

At your (lack) of systems.

You see, once you begin to understand the key differences between profit, personal income, taxes, and the flow of money into and through your pest control business, you can begin to make money.

Literally.

In fact, that was one of the biggest "ah-has" I had on my own journey in the pest control industry: If I wanted to boost my personal income, our company profits, and our cash flow through the business, I had three choices – and you do too.

You can charge more for your services.

You can reduce your expenses.

Some combination of both of these.

In the home services industry, the simple fact is payroll is generally the biggest expense. In order to reduce expenses by any measurable amount, I'd have to lay people off or pay them less.

Let me assure you, that's rarely ever an option!

In reality, when I was faced with this decision, I chose to pay higher than average wages, not because I was looking for "better" people, but because it generally lowers turnover in the long run. Fewer new hires mean lower training expenses. Sure, we spend a bit more each week, but the men and women in our company stay longer and perform at a higher level, and I've got the data to prove it.

For example, last year, even with all the uncertainty around Covid, the wage increases we paid as a company totaled over $350,000. Even more exciting? These increases were based on the profits our teams were helping us to generate!

That higher level of operator results in higher perceived value in the field – and remember, neither Michael nor I suggest hiring people who are exceptionally skilled people, just people who are willing to learn and utilize an exceptional system.

This higher level of service provides us with the opportunity to charge more. That first option I mentioned above, remember?

There's more to it than simply raising your rates though. As we began to do this in the company, we also began to look at what other services we could add. This inevitably led me down a lot of rabbit holes, but the work also showed where we could add value in other aspects of their lives.

We experimented with additional pest control services – bedbugs, termites, bees, and other "emergency" items. We explored commercial and industrial services, and we allocated money in our budgets to investigate growth areas such as technology and employee care.

The point in all this is simple: Until you make the time to understand the flow of money through your business, and the subsequent effects it has on profits and income, you can't really quantify how successful your own efforts will be. More importantly, you'll be cut off and removed from the last, and arguably most important point of Michael's four types of money: Equity.

Creating a Strategy for Equity

By now you might be thinking, "Could it really be this simple? Could the key to building a successful pest control business really just be understanding the actual prices and costs of doing business?"

To a degree, the answer is a resounding, "Yes!"

…But income, profit, and cashflow is really nothing without equity.

As Michael said, equity is simply the value of your pest control business, and far too many owners never allow themselves to build equity.

Lean in close because the secret is in the strategy.

You have to begin with the end in mind.

I've already touched on this point earlier, as we talked about taxes and profits. Personally, I knew we wanted to end our fiscal years with not only healthy profit margins, but also, cash reserves. To do that, I had to determine what steps we needed to take to achieve smaller, individual financial goals. With those weekly or monthly goals in place, we could simply forecast forward to an annual goal, or we could look at annual goals and reverse engineer quarterly, monthly, or weekly goals.

Equity isn't just made on paper, it's also made by taking a long, hard look at costs.

I learned how to do more with less.

We canceled subscriptions that didn't serve us, or that didn't meet the standards I set for value. I began looking at how to create internal jobs rather than outsourced ones. Of course, this is where having the right people began to pay off too.

It became my own personal habit NOT to "do" the financial work – that's strategic and tactical work for bookkeepers and CPAs - but to dive into our financial statements such as cashflow, profit and loss, and so on – and ask questions about them.

My goal, unlike so many pest control business owners, became understanding why we spent the money we did. If there was a good reason, that was fine, but I was very focused on understanding where the money went, and the value it provided us.

That's an important thing to remember. You won't always reduce your spending. Just as I had no qualms about paying higher wages for the right people, I didn't (and you shouldn't) have any problem allocating money in your budget to resources that will improve your business and its operations.

The Long View

Change – at least in terms of money – doesn't happen over- night. There is a learning curve; there will be mistakes; there will be dead ends; and eventually, there will be breakthroughs.

Each year, the needle moves a little more.

Each year, the profits become a little larger.

Personally, it took nearly seven years of growing beyond the mindset of a technician to feel comfortable to wear the title of a true entrepreneur in the conversation about money in my own business.

It might be like that for you too.

The truth is, the systems and ideas you need aren't new, they've been around for scores of years. What IS new is how you choose to look at the money you make and the money you spend within your pest control business.

I think of it in terms of where you wish to spend your time. You can continue to run the business like an ATM, constantly taking cash out and worrying about when the money will run out (and it will), or you can spend the time to think of and create the systems within your business to not only pay you for the work you do, but also to handle all the expenses the business has. The secret is simple: either choice takes the same amount of work!

If you choose to ignore a profit strategy, you'll be left with a business you've spent years to grow that is worth no more than the tools and equipment you own. If you begin to actively manage profits, accept the fact you can't "avoid" taxes, and really dig into the financials of your company, when the time comes to sell your business (and it will, either because you're retiring, dead, or exhausted), you'll have something of real value to show for your years of hard work.

By ignoring money, you create a money strategy, and by focusing on money, you create a money strategy. In the end though, the results are far more rewarding when you take the time to address the money head on. ✤

On the Subject of Planning

Michael E. Gerber

People in an organization operating from a creative mode . . . approach planning first by determining what they truly want to create, thus in essence becoming true to themselves.

—Robert Fritz, The Path of Least Resistance

Another obvious oversight revealed in Steve and Peggy's story was the absence of true planning.

Every contractor starting his or her own business must have a plan. You should never begin to see customers without a plan in place. But, like Steve, most contractors do exactly that.

A pest control contractor lacking a vision is simply someone who goes to work every day. Someone who is just doing it, doing it, doing it. Busy, busy, busy. Maybe making money, maybe not. Maybe getting something out of life, maybe not. Taking chances without really taking control.

The plan tells anyone who needs to know *how we do things here.* The plan defines the objective and the process by which you will attain it. The plan encourages you to organize tasks into functions, and then helps people grasp the logic of each of those functions. This in turn permits you to bring new employees up to speed quickly.

There are numerous books and seminars on the subject of pest control and all its related aspects, but they focus on the technical aspects of making you a better pest control technician. I want to teach you something that you've never been taught before: how to be a manager. It has nothing to do with conventional business management and everything to do with thinking like an entrepreneur.

The Planning Triangle

As we discussed in the Preface, every pest control sole proprietorship is a business, every pest control business is a company, and every pest control company is an enterprise. The trouble with most companies owned by a pest control technician is that they are dependent on the technician. That's because they're a sole proprietorship—the smallest, most limited form a company can take. Businesses are formed around the expert technician – the man or woman who's out in the field every day, spraying homes and businesses.

You may choose in the beginning to form a sole proprietorship, but you should understand its limitations. The company called a *sole proprietorship* depends on the owner—that is, the technician. The company called a *business* depends on other people plus a system by which that business does what it does. Once your sole proprietorship becomes a business, you can replicate it, turning it into an *enterprise*.

Consider the example of Sea Pest Control. The customers don't call asking for Douglas Sea, although he is one of the top pest control contractors around. After all, he can only handle so many calls a day and be in only one location at a time.

Yet he wants to offer his high-quality services to more people in the community. If he has reliable systems in place—systems that any qualified field technician can learn to use—he has created a business and it can be replicated. Douglas can then go on to offer his services—which demand his guidance, not his presence—in a multitude of different settings. He can open dozens of pest control businesses, none of which need Douglas Sea himself, except in the role of entrepreneur.

Is your pest control company going to be a sole proprietorship, a business, or an enterprise? Planning is crucial to answering this all-important question. Whatever you choose to do must be communicated by your plan, which is really three interrelated plans in one. We call it the Planning Triangle, and it consists of:

- The business plan
- The service plan
- The completion plan

The three plans form a triangle, with the business plan at the base, the service plan in the center, and the completion plan at the apex.

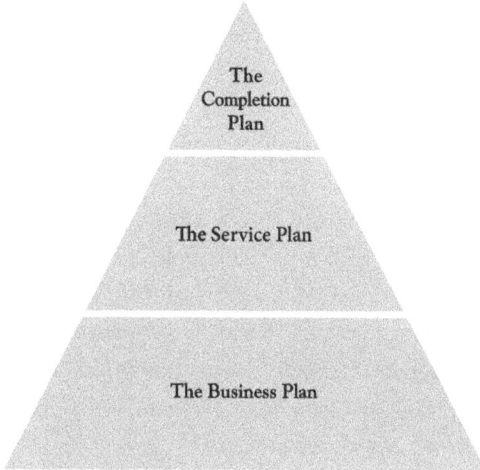

The business plan determines *who* you are (the business), the service plan determines *what* you do (the specific focus of your pest control business), and the completion plan determines *how* you do it (the fulfillment process).

By looking at the Planning Triangle, we see that the three critical plans are interconnected. The connection between them is established by asking the following questions:

1.   Who are we?
2.   What do we do?
3.   How do we do it?

Who are we? is purely a strategic question.

What do we do? is both a strategic and a tactical question.

How do we do it? is both a strategic and a tactical question.

Strategic questions shape the vision and destiny of your business, of which your service is only one essential component. Tactical questions turn that vision into reality. Thus, strategic questions provide the foundation for tactical questions, just as the base provides the foundation for the middle and apex of your Planning Triangle.

First ask: What do we do and how do we do it ... *strategically?*

And then: What do we do and how do we do it ... *practically?*

Let's look at how the three plans will help you develop your service.

The Business Plan

Your business plan will determine what you choose to do in your pest control company and the way you choose to do it. Without a business plan, your company can do little more than survive. And even that will take more than a little luck.

Without a business plan, you're treading water in a deep pool with no shore in sight. You're working against the natural flow.

I'm not talking about the traditional business plan that is taught in business schools. No, this business plan reads like a story—the most important story you will ever tell.

Your business plan must clearly describe

•   the business you are creating;
•   the purpose it will serve;
•   the vision it will pursue;
•   the process through which you will turn that vision into a reality; and

- the way money will be used to realize your vision.

Build your business plan with *business* language, not *technical* language (the language of the pest control industry). Make sure the plan focuses on matters of interest to your lenders and shareholders rather than just your technicians. It should rely on demographics and psychographics to tell you who buys and why; it should also include projections for return on investment and return on equity. Use it to detail both the market and the strategy through which you intend to become a leader in that market, not as a pest control sole proprietorship but as a business enterprise.

The business plan, though absolutely essential, is only one of three critical plans every contractor needs to create and implement. Now let's take a look at the three legs of the business plan.

The Service Plan

The service plan includes everything a pest control contractor needs to know, have, and do in order to deliver his or her promise to a customer on time, every time.

Every task should prompt you to ask three questions:

1. What do I need to know?
2. What do I need to have?
3. What do I need to do?

What Do I Need to *Know?*

What information do I need to satisfy my promise on time, every time, exactly as promised? In order to recognize what you need to know, you must understand the expectations and limitations of others, including your customers, administrators, technicians, and other employees. Are you clear on those expectations? Don't make the mistake of assuming you know. Instead, create a need-to-know checklist to make sure you ask all the necessary questions.

A need-to-know checklist might look like this:
- What are the expectations of my customers?
- What are the expectations of my technicians?
- What are the expectations of my staff?
- What are the expectations of my vendors?

What Do I Need to *Have?*

This question raises the issue of resources—namely, money, people, and time. If you don't have enough money to finance operations, how can you fulfill those expectations without creating cash-flow problems? If you don't have enough trained people, what happens then? And if you don't have enough time to manage your business, what happens when you can't be in two places at once?

Don't assume that you can get what you need when you need it. Most often, you can't. And even if you can get what you need at the last minute, you'll pay dearly for it.

What Do I Need to *Do?*

The focus here is on actions to be started and finished. What do I need to do to fulfill the expectations of this customer on time, every time, exactly as promised? For example, what exactly are the steps to ensure the customer has a comfortable and consistent temperature in every room of the home?

Your customers fall into distinct categories, and those categories make up your business. The best pest control businesses will invariably focus on fewer and fewer categories as they discover the importance of doing one thing better than anyone else.

Answering the question *What do I need to do?* demands a series of action plans, including:
- the objective to be achieved;

- the standards by which you will know that the objective has been achieved;
- the benchmarks you need to read in order for the objective to be achieved;
- the function/person accountable for the completion of the benchmarks;
- the budget for the completion of each benchmark; and
- the time by which each benchmark must be completed.

Your action plans become the foundation for the Completion Plan. And the reason you need completion plans is to ensure that everything you do is not only realistic but can also be managed.

The Completion Plan

If The Business Plan gives you results and provides you with standards, The Completion Plan tells you everything you need to know about every benchmark in The Service Plan—that is, how you're going to fulfill customer expectations on time, every time, as promised. In other words, how you're going to ensure the customer's airflow is consistent in every room, set a thermostat for optimal energy saving, or educate a customer about the importance of regularly servicing their ducts and filters.

The Completion Plan is essentially the operations manual, providing information about the details of doing tactical work. It is a guide to tell the people responsible for doing that work exactly how to do it.

Every completion plan becomes a part of the knowledge base of your business. No completion plan goes to waste. Every completion plan becomes a kind of textbook that explains to new employees or new associates joining your team how your business operates in a way that distinguishes it from all other pest control businesses.

To return to an earlier example, The Completion Plan for making a Big Mac is explicitly described in the *McDonald's*

Operation Manual, as is every completion plan needed to run a McDonald's business.

The Completion Plan for a pest control technician might include the step-by-step details of how to assess a customer's home, or crawl-space, or yard—in contrast to how everyone else has learned to do it. Of course, all those who work in pest control industry "know" how to do this, BUT they've learned to do it the same way everyone else has learned to do it. If you are going to stand out as unique in the minds of your customers, employees, and others, you must invent your own way of doing even ordinary things. Most of that value-added perception will come from your communication skills, your listening skills, and your innovative skills in transforming an ordinary visit into a customer experience.

Perhaps you'll decide that a mandatory part of new client analysis is to sketch a quick map of the location using a digital or Bluetooth measuring device and a tablet, explaining the different measurements to the prospect so that she has a better understanding of the analysis of her home. If no other contractor your customer has seen has ever taken the time to explain how pests move through a space based on temperature or moisture levels, you'll immediately set yourself apart. You must constantly raise the questions: *How do we do it here? How* should *we do it here?*

The quality of your answers will determine how effectively you distinguish your business from every other pest control business.

Benchmarks

You can measure the movement of your business—from what it is today to what it will be in the future—using business benchmarks. These are the goals you want your business to achieve during its lifetime.

Your benchmarks should include the following:
- Financial benchmarks

- Emotional benchmarks (the impact your business will have on everyone who comes into contact with it)
- Performance benchmarks
- Customer benchmarks (Who are they? Why do they come to you? What will your business give them that no one else will?)
- Employee benchmarks (How do you grow people? How do you find people who want to grow? How do you create a school in your business that will teach your people skills they can't learn anywhere else?)

Your business benchmarks will reflect (1) the position your business will hold in the minds and hearts of your customers, employees, and investors, and (2) how you intend to make that position a reality through the systems you develop.

Your benchmarks will describe how your management team will take shape and what systems you will need to develop so that your managers, just like McDonald's managers, will be able to produce the results for which they will be held accountable.

Benefits of the Planning Triangle

By implementing the Planning Triangle, you will discover

- What your business will look, act, and feel like when it's fully evolved;
- When that's going to happen
- How much money you will make

These, then, are the primary purposes of the three critical plans: (1) to clarify precisely what needs to be done to get what the contractor wants from his or her business and life, and (2) to define the specific steps by which it will happen.

First *this* must happen, *then* that must happen. One, two, three. By monitoring your progress, step by step, you can determine whether you're on the right track.

That's what planning is all about. It's about creating a standard—a yardstick—against which you will be able to measure your performance.

Failing to create such a standard is like throwing a straw into a hurricane. Who knows where that straw will land?

Have you taken the leap? Have you accepted that the word *business* and the word *sole proprietorship* are not synonymous? That a sole proprietorship relies on the owner and a business relies on other people plus a system?

Because most contractors are control freaks, 99 percent of today's pest control companies are sole proprietorships, not businesses.

The result, as a friend of mine says, is that "contractors are spending all day stamping out fires when all around them the forest is ablaze. They're out of touch, and that contractor better take control of the business before someone else does."

Because contractors are never taught to think like businesspeople, the skilled tradesperson is forever at war with the businessperson. This is especially evident in large pest control companies, where bureaucrats (businesspeople) often try to control contractors (field technicians). They usually end up treating each other as combatants. In fact, the single greatest reason contractors become entrepreneurs is to divorce such bureaucrats and to begin to reinvent the pest control enterprise.

That's you. Now the divorce is over and a new love affair has begun. You're a pest control contractor with a plan! Who wouldn't want to do business with such a person?

Now let's take the next step in our strategic odyssey. Let's take a closer look at the subject of *management*. But before we do, let's read what Austin has to say on the subject of *planning*. ✤

The Problem with Planning

Austin Clark

"Unless commitment is made, there are only promises and hopes; but no plans."

— Peter F. Drucker

I imagine you've heard the old saying, "If you fail to plan, you plan to fail."

There's no doubt this is true, but in my experience, too many owners and operators in the pest control world confuse "plans" with "goals."

You might have the *goal* of a million—dollar business, but without a *plan* to bring that into reality, what you've really got is simply a daydream. Now, this might simply be me playing with words, but if you want to bring your dreams, plans, and goals into reality, then you've got to be ultra-specific, ultra-focused, and dedicated to making sure they happen, no matter what you want to call them.

For our purposes here though, let's separate goals from plans.

A goal is simply a place or thing you've heard about and think you might need to check out.

A million dollars.

A Hawaiian vacation.

A big house in the right neighborhood.

Getting in shape.

A million dollars is simply a number. Hawaii is simply a place. That big house is simply a building. Getting in shape is simply a number on a scale or the size of the waistband on your pants.

By itself, in our definition, a goal means nothing. Remember the short conversation between Alice and the Cheshire Cat in Lewis Carroll's *Alice in Wonderland?*

Alice, coming to a fork in the road, asked the Cheshire Cat, "Would you tell me, please, which way I ought to go from here?"

"That depends a good deal on where you want to get to."

Young Alice responded, "I don't much care where."

The Cheshire Cat smiled his big smile and said, "Then it doesn't much matter which way you go...."

That's where "goals" take you...

A plan though?

A plan can give us something to work with.

How we'll make those million dollars, how we get to Hawaii, what we'll do in that house, and the actions we can take to fit back into those comfortable jeans we've kept in the closet for too long.

Like many of us, I haven't been very good at reaching the goals I set for myself, even though I've long been in the habit of writing them down. Nonetheless, I've recorded hundreds of them over the years, and even tried to review them periodically to check in on my progress.

It's interesting to see how my approach to goals – specifically the plans I'll put in place to reach them – have changed in the last decade. As I write this, I'm looking over one of my old notebooks where those goals were carefully written, and I can see why so many of them were never achieved – I never took the time to plan how to reach them.

Now this book isn't about how or why I never became a master at cooking fish (yep, I wrote that one down about eight years ago...), but it IS about understanding the goals you set in your business ... and how you can achieve them.

In the last chapter, Michael shared his Planning Triangle, and how it can absolutely change the way you think about your pest control business. I'd like to take a deeper dive into that.

No matter where you are in the Planning Triangle – Business Plan, Practice Plan, or the Completion Plan – it's imperative you get out of your own way. To truly apply the ideas of the E-Myth to your pest control business, you cannot allow yourself to be stuck in the Tactical Work - the daily work of the business.

The work of the Technicians. The work of the Managers.

I recognize you might be among the many thousands of truly small pest control companies out there: one man and a truck, perhaps your spouse or a family member helps with billing and scheduling, or you have an assistant who handles that while you do the actual work of the business – pest control.

That doesn't mean you can't create a plan.

It also means that most – if not ALL – of the marketing and training you see that applies to our business today is useless to you, as an entrepreneur.

It's designed to make *Technicians* more efficient.
- How to get more clients
- How to do more today
- How to upsell your clients when you're in their home
- How to automate this process or that one
- How to be two places at once
- And so on, and so on, and so on...

Basically, everything you see or read about our industry is about how to squeeze thirty hours out of each day.

You. Cannot. Do.That.

Your Business Plan reflects that reality.

Your Practice Plan plots your course for stepping into the role of a leader within your business.

The Completion Plan reliably demonstrates how your business operates.

All of these work together to help you achieve the goals you've set – and that doesn't matter if you're "one man and a truck" or your pest control company will generate several million dollars in sales this year and you have a team of technicians and a management staff.

...In the end, the Planning Triangle will be the roadmap your pest control business follows, and it all must start with one simple action.

Keep A Record

This is where most pest control owners stop before they ever start. They mistakenly think that any plan must be beautifully formatted, free of any errors or omissions, and a misspelled word or lined out note is somehow a condemnation of their ability to plan.

THAT is the real mistake.

Just as I shared with you earlier my own goals and my inability to achieve them in many cases, the first step is to understand those goals, and the planning they require to make them a reality.

You don't need a fancy spreadsheet with your business name and logo on it to create a plan. I still use a Google Doc, but I know other successful pest control owners who use different tools and more than a few that begin any plan with a simple clean sheet of paper and a beginner's mind.

So where do you begin with this clean sheet of paper?

At the bottom of the Planning Triangle, with the Business Plan your pest control company will follow. Now, this isn't the business plan the SBA wants you to send them if you're going to take out a loan, it's really the outline of what exactly your business does.

The impact it will have on your clients and customers, the results it will provide to investors and stakeholders, and – don't forget this one – how this business serves your own dreams, visions, and yes, goals.

It's the reason you're in business and the results the business will achieve.

Let me tell you what your Business Plan *isn't*: It's not the work you do every day and have done year after year. That's why planning – the way we're doing it here - is so "hard."

Within your Business Plan, you're beginning to do the real work of entrepreneurship, perhaps for the first time. All the planning in the world does you no good until you act on it, which is why the very first step of the Planning Triangle is to look inward to your own motivations and outward past the daily work. Ask yourself the right questions, and really look for the answers.

Why are you doing this? Where do you wish to go? What will you achieve this year? In three years? In five?

What don't you like about the work you do?

This is the real work of the entrepreneur, to understand where you want your business to go and the people who will benefit from your hard work.

Until you do that, you'll never be able to move the needle. These are, in essence, the foundation of the work you have to do in the Business Plan, as Michael outlined earlier.

Now is the time to begin fixing that, and the Planning Triangle is the beginning.

Write it down. Document it. Measure it.

Stay On Course

When you move into the Practice Plan, you might find yourself confronted, as I did, by the fact I never really thought about the work I did in my own business.

I just *did* it.

Maybe you can relate? When and if you've ever hired someone to do this job, more than likely you simply had them ride along with you and "do what I do." From those two or three days, they either "got it" or they didn't, and even if they didn't, you probably figured they were good enough and you could simply fix whatever they didn't do properly.

The same thing with your bookkeeper. Your receptionist. Your payroll and accounts payable and marketing and ordering and on, and on, and on.

Now is the time to begin fixing that, and the Practice Plan is the beginning.

Here is the place you begin to really dig in to take a more detailed look into the components of the pest control business – *your* pest control business – and see the things it needs.

For me, this meant understanding not only what our core offer was – pest control – but also, what that actually meant. Did we want to handle emergencies like bees, or bedbugs, or a venomous snake in the dining room?

How would we charge for those services? How did we communicate with our clients?

Would our products include annual contracts, or termites, or were there additional services we could offer (or partner with other companies) to handle for our clients?

What, exactly, did we *do*, and how did we do it? More importantly, were we doing it "right?" You and I both know that you can send three different technicians to a house and the customer will have three completely different experiences.

Now is the time to decide which one is the right one. (Here's a hint – it doesn't matter what YOU think, it's how the customer perceives it.) As you go through the Practice Plan, you have to ask the same three questions Michael asked in the last chapter:

• What do I need to know?
• What do I need to have?
• What do I need to do?

You're asking these questions of EVERYTHING in the business – not as the owner, but as the person doing that particular job or task. You are beginning to form a picture of the tools, the skills, the abilities, and the time that will be needed for any reasonable person to do that work.

...And it's not necessarily YOU!

I can't stress that enough. As you create your Practice Plan, you have to remove all the experience you have, you have to take things off of autopilot, and you have to unpack your experience and get out of your own way.

It's where you *document* and prove that it takes 45 minutes to service 1,500 square feet of residential space. Where you verify that a technician needs *these* tools and *these* supplies on the truck every day, but, due to traffic conditions in your town, a technician can only make eight service calls each day.

The Practice Plan is NOT just the technical side of the pest control business either. As you go through this planning process, you'll look at how and where money comes into and out of your business, and when. You'll look at how much you spend – and actually consume – in supplies, and the costs of having those supplies on the shelf instead of cash reserves in the bank.

This is where you discover (or rediscover) the metrics of your business, your region, and your particular offers. Not only that, but where you'll specifically address the Key Performance Indicators (KPIs) that drive customer satisfaction, conversions, additional services, profits, and every other measurable data point of your pest control business.

How far down the rabbit hole should you go?

As far as you can. Seriously! While it might sound extreme, Michael once tested the effects the color of his suit had on sales! A brown suit didn't generate as many sales as a blue suit! Think about that when you think about the uniform your technicians wear, or the color of your trucks.

In short, the Practice Plan is where you actually learn how your pest control business really runs and what makes it run better.

On To Completion

For an organizer like me, tracking down this type of data is second nature, especially after the payroll fiasco I shared earlier. On the other hand, for you, it might not be as easy. As I've talked with pest control owners over the years and shared our results and strategies, two groups of people have emerged.

The first one is shocked that we've found the time to actually get these types of metrics for our business and customers. The second assures me they "already know all that…" and tries to change the subject.

Either one is the wrong way to view the challenge of planning because all this work you're doing – from documenting cash flow to the metrics of service to how efficiently you can run a service call - is designed to give you data.

The data you need to grow your pest control business, to hire the right team, to allow you to get off the merry-go-round of trying to play too many roles in your company. Your Business Plan and Practice Plan will give you the foundation to create the plan that can truly run your entire pest control business … the Completion Plan.

Seriously. Until you'll take the time to do this type of planning though, your pest control business will only ever give you a living, not a life.

I'm not going to lie to you, it's hard to stay motivated to keep doing this – constantly asking questions, constantly trying to document the "why" of a result, and constantly planning and testing the conclusions you've been able to make. If you've got a team, even if it's only one or two part-time people, then there are parts of the plan you can delegate to them.

It might be something as simple as asking them to document the tasks they do each day or logging the steps they have to take to make an order, or schedule an appointment, or even how they answer the phone. Unfortunately, you're not going to be able to delegate it all.

You're going to have to do some work, and it's not always pleasant.

Where does all this documentation go? Ultimately, into an Operations Manual each of these plans is helping you to create for your pest control business. Within that, you'll also be deciding how do you train people. What, exactly, is that process? Videos? A workbook? A series of benchmarks done via system (not just the old "on the job" training many of us received, either. You cannot "train" anyone by teaching them to "just do what I do...") Up until that point, though, it doesn't matter if you've got all your plans on a legal pad, a Google Doc, or even an Excel spreadsheet – as long as you've taken the time to do the work.

Here's the thing though: remember those goals we talked about at the beginning of this chapter? If some of those goals revolve around things like free time, or vacations with your family, or providing more financial opportunities to your kids and grandkids than you had, you're not going to achieve those continuing down the path you're on right now.

As Henry Ford was quoted as saying, "Whether you think you can or you can't, you're right."

Dig into your business and the goals you have for it using the ideas that Michael and I are sharing. You'll be surprised how quickly you not only solidify the goals you want; you will see how quickly you can create a plan for your pest control company, and also an operations plan that allows you to shift your role from that of a technician who built himself a job to that of an entrepreneur who has built a business. ✤

On the Subject of Management

Michael E. Gerber

The most important figures that one needs for management are unknown or unknowable, but successful management must nevertheless take account of them.

—W. Edwards Deming

E very small business owner, including Steve Walsh from our story, eventually faces the issues of management. Most face it badly.

Why do so many contractors suffer from a kind of paralysis when it comes to dealing with management? Why are so few able to get their pest control business to work the way they want it to and to run it on time? Why are their managers (if they have any) seemingly so inept?

There are two main problems. First, the contractor usually abdicates accountability for management by hiring an office manager. Thus, the contractor is working hand in glove with someone who is supposed to do the managing. But the contractor is unmanageable himself!

The contractor doesn't think like a manager because he doesn't think he *is* a manager. He's a pest control contractor! He rules the roost. And so he gets the office manager to take care of stuff like scheduling appointments, keeping his calendar, collecting receivables, hiring/firing, and much more.

Second, no matter who does the managing, they usually have a completely dysfunctional idea of what it means to manage. They're trying to manage people, contrary to what is needed.

We often hear that a good manager must be a "people person." Someone who loves to nourish, figure out, support, care for, teach, baby, monitor, mentor, direct, track, motivate, and, if all else fails, threaten or beat up her people.

Don't believe it. Management has far less to do with people than you've been led to believe.

In fact, despite the claims of every management book written by management gurus (who have seldom managed anything), no one—with the exception of a few bloodthirsty tyrants—has ever learned how to manage people.

And the reason is simple: People are almost impossible to manage.

Yes, it's true. People are unmanageable. They're inconsistent, unpredictable, unchangeable, unrepentant, irrepressible, and generally impossible.

Doesn't knowing this make you feel better? Now you understand why you've had all those problems! Do you feel the relief, the heavy stone lifted from your chest?

The time has come to fully understand what management is really all about. Rather than managing *people*, management is really all about managing a *process*, a step-by-step way of doing things, which, combined with other processes, becomes a system. For example:

- The Process for on-time scheduling
- The Process for answering the telephone
- The Process for greeting a customer
- The Process for organizing customer files

Thus, a process is the step-by-step way of doing something over time. Considered as a whole, these processes are a system:

- The On-time Scheduling System
- The Telephone Answering System
- The Customer Greeting System
- The File Organization System

Instead of managing people, then, the truly effective manager has been taught a System for managing a Process through which People get things done.

More precisely, managers and their people, *together*, manage the processes—the Systems—that comprise your business. Management is less about *who* gets things done in your business than about *how* things get done.

In fact, great managers are not fascinated with people, as our contemporary mantra suggests we must be, but instead, with how things get done through people using extraordinarily effective Systems to do it.

To do that, great managers constantly ask themselves and their people key questions, such as:

- What is the result we intend to produce?
- Are we producing that result every single time?
- If we're not producing that result every single time, why not?
- If we are producing that result every single time, how could we produce even better results?
- Do we lack a system? If so, what would that system look like if we were to create it?
- If we have a system, why aren't we using it?

And so forth.

In short, a great manager can leave the office fully assured that it will run at least as well as it does when he or she is physically in the room.

Great managers are those who use a great management system. A system that shouts, "This is *how* we manage here." Not, "This is *who* manages here."

In a truly effective company, *how* you manage is always more important than *who* manages. Provided a system is in place, how you manage is transferable, whereas who manages isn't. *How* you manage can be taught, whereas *who* manages can't be.

When a company is dependent on *who* manages—Katie, Kim, or Kevin—that business is in serious jeopardy. Because when Katie, Kim, or Kevin leaves, that business has to start over again. What an enormous waste of time and resources!

Even worse, when a company is dependent on *who* manages, you can bet all the managers in that business are doing their own thing. What could be more unproductive than ten managers who each manage in a unique way? How in the world could you possible manage those managers?

The answer is: You can't. Because it takes you right back to trying to manage *people* again.

And, as I hope you now know, that's impossible.

In this chapter, I often refer to managers in the plural. I know that most pest control contractors only have one manager—the office manager. And so you may be thinking that a management system isn't so important in a small pest control business. After all, the office manager does whatever an office manager does (and thank God because you don't want to do it). Why go through the trouble of creating a Management System?

But if your sole proprietorship is ever going to turn into the business it could become, and if that business is ever going to turn into the enterprise of your dreams, then the questions you ask about how the office manager manages your affairs are critical ones. Because until you come to grips with your dual role as owner and key employee, and the relationship your manager has to those two roles, your sole proprietorship/business/enterprise will never realize its potential. Thus the need for a Management System.

Management System

What, then, is a Management System?

The E-Myth says that a Management System is the method by which every manager innovates, quantifies, orchestrates, and then monitors the systems through which your service produces the results you expect.

According to the E-Myth, a manager's job is simple:

A manager's job is to invent the Systems through which the owner's vision is consistently and faithfully manifested at the operating level of the business.

Which brings us right back to the purpose of your business and the need for an entrepreneurial vision.

Are you beginning to see what I'm trying to share with you? That your business is *one single thing*? And that all the subjects we're discussing here—money, planning, management, and so on—are all about doing one thing well?

That one thing is the one thing your service is intended to do: distinguish your pest control business from all others.

It is the manager's role to make certain it all fits. And it's your role as entrepreneur to make sure your manager knows what the business is supposed to look, act, and feel like when it's finally done. As clearly as you know how, you must convey to your manager what you know to be true—your vision, your picture of the business when it's finally done. In this way, your vision is translated into your manager's marching orders every day he or she reports to work.

Unless that vision is embraced by your manager, you and your people will suffer from the tyranny of routine. And your business will suffer from it, too.

Now let's move on to *people*. Because, as we know, it's people who are causing all our problems. But first let's read what Austin has to say about *management*. ✤

Management by Transparency and Accountability

Austin Clark

"A manager is a guide. He takes a group of people and says,
'With you, I can make us a success; I can show you the way.'"
—Arsene Wenger

It's been said – and I firmly believe – that people don't quit jobs, they quit managers. In my own experience in the pest control industry, the biggest contributor to the title of "bad manager" is simply a lack of understanding how to do the job of managing.

Think about it: who gets that promotion to "manager?"

A lot of times, it's a technician, or the owner, or, in some cases, you might hire someone from a completely different industry to be the "office manager."

We both know what happens then. The owner gives the new manager a little guidance, tells them a fraction of what the job actually entails (probably because the owner isn't even sure of what – or when – something needs to be done), and the expectation is the manager will "learn as they go."

Rationalize it any way you want to, but the result is the same – you've thrown them to the wolves. At the very least, you've set them up to have a lot of surprise tasks they'll be called upon to do at the last minute, or after a deadline. You've also paralyzed them from being able to actually do the very things you want them to do because you never taught them and you never created the system for them to learn!

Who wants a job like that?

Let me tell you, no one you want managing your pest control business!

I'll be the first to tell you, I've been as guilty as anyone of this same thinking. About six years ago, we had an applicant that really opened my eyes. Her name isn't important, but for now, let's call her Sarah. Sarah ACED the interview; she'd previously worked for a company I considered an industry leader in pest control and was looking for a change.

As you can imagine, we were thrilled to have such a qualified candidate, and we hired her.

Forty-eight hours later, Sarah quit.

You can imagine how that felt. Losing great people is never easy, and the worst part was I simply couldn't understand how we could have failed so fast. At that time, we were growing quickly, but I felt we had a replicable process in place, but no matter, we failed Sarah, and I never saw it coming.

Well, most of us can rationalize things, and I'm no exception.

It'd be easy to say Sarah might just not want to be in the pest control business, or she was having trouble elsewhere in her life and we were simply collateral damage due to another problem. However, her quitting so suddenly caught me off guard, and it really made me dig into not only why we failed her, but how.

I've made thousands of mistakes in operating my company, and today, I'm not ashamed to say that many of the people who have left us left because of me. That's nothing to be proud of, but it's how I feel, and I can't help but feel that many of those people who left of their own free will might have stayed if we'd been a little better here or done things differently there.

What I've learned as a manager, from Sarah and many others, is that we've got to have systems and processes in place. It helps every person on the team know what to do, how to do it, and to feel good about the skills they have and the ones they are still developing. Michael said it best in the last chapter when he mentioned that people are, ultimately, unmanageable.

That's a hard truth for many of us to swallow, but it is the truth. Imagine though, when you build a system that brings out the very best in people and supports them to do extraordinary work.

THAT was the real learning experience with Sarah. Until then, I'd been casually committed to building systems and processes in the company and aimed our hiring systems on finding the "right" people. As it turns out, the smarter way to manage my pest control company was far easier – create the system that made quality people into the "right' people.

Don't try to hire experts to run your system.

The Value Add

There are a lot of ways to improve the management systems in your pest control business, but if you really want to move the needle, you have to look at how each piece of the puzzle adds value.

To your people. To your clients. To your organization.

I'm not simply talking about monetary value, although the right management system does do that. I'm talking about removing the stumbling blocks that impact your company in terms of getting the job done.

What can you do to allow your team to get the job done faster? More effectively? More efficiently?

What can you do to make it easier for your customers to give you money? To schedule services? To make sure they don't have to worry about anything related to "pest control" ever again?

It might seem callous to say this, but what systems and processes do you need in place to take "thinking" or "worrying" or "I don't know" out of your business conversations? Let me give you an example that's near and dear to Michael's heart... McDonalds' hamburgers versus you cooking burgers on the grill at home.

Now you might be thinking, "Austin, my burgers are WAY better than McDonalds!"

You might be right, but in terms of managing those two processes, which one is easier?

McDonalds has a system, perfected over nearly eighty years, and billions of successful examples. You pull in, you give them your order, you pay them, they give you a bag filled with burgers and piping hot French fries, and those extra napkins you asked for.

Plus, an ice-cold coke.

Meanwhile, to cook those burgers in your backyard tonight, you're sending a grocery list to your spouse you've added to two times already; you've forgotten the charcoal (or you're out of propane); the ground beef is still a little frozen; it takes fifteen minutes to get all the buns toasted; the burgers are getting cold while you wait; this one isn't cooked enough; that one is burned; and, despite the three texts you sent your teenager when they ran to the store, they bought the wrong kind of pickles.

Let me tell you, my friend, in my experience, most pest control businesses are managed a LOT more like an ad-hoc backyard barbeque than a well-organized services business.

Or a "simple" hamburger stand.

The bigger point is, when there's a mistake in your order at McDonalds, they've got a way to fix it. If you make one cooking your "burgers," you've got to get personally involved and create a solution on the fly.

...And as a manager, you and your people are going to make mistakes, so why not ensure that the processes and systems that support your pest control company also make it easy for everyone involved to do the right thing?

Owning the Good and the Bad

On the surface, it's not particularly difficult to create the systems you need to effectively manage a pest control business.

There's scheduling, marketing, sales, hiring, A/R, A/P, ordering, and so on. You might have those systems in place, or you might not.

Based on conversations with hundreds of owners over the years, many smaller pest control businesses are relying on the experience of their people and an office manager that's always moving at the speed of sound.

That's a problem waiting to happen.

Michael's already shared a lot of ways you can sort out the management processes, so I don't want to simply restate that now. I want to look at the real management challenges we all face and that can't always be systemized – mistakes.

If there's one thing customers don't like, it's mistakes. Maybe your technician got stuck in traffic, maybe the address was wrong, maybe the scheduling system failed. In my own business, our team knows we can never account for every situation, but we can prepare for them, so we developed what we call our Accountability Board and an Error Log.

I'll share more about it in a later chapter, but the whole point of this system is to identify recurring errors – no matter where they might originate. This gives us an easy way – a process – to track and monitor our existing systems AND to identify areas where a system might need to be created or modified to reflect new trends.

Let me give you an example: most pest control companies, especially the smallest ones, make collecting payments far too hard.

They take checks, they send invoices through the mail, and they wait.

And wait.

And wait some more.

People are busy, invoices get lost; sure, some people "forget" to pay, but the end result is the money YOUR company earned isn't in the bank account.

But you've already paid your technician. You've paid for the chemicals. You've paid for the truck.

…And your client simply forgot to pay that one paper invoice you sent days after your technician treated the house.

The Error Log is our way to catch those problems and document them. It's simply a Google Form anyone can fill out. Maybe it's a technician who doesn't have enough time to safely make the drive between jobs, or another technician who's found that it's virtually impossible to get from this neighborhood to that one before eleven o'clock due to a road construction project.

ANY incident can be added to the Error Log, which automatically populates to a larger spreadsheet, which, in our case, is the Accountability Board.

So, in the case of slow accounts receivable, our bookkeeping team might notice that A/R is taking longer than usual and document this in the Error Log. From there, the trend could be recognized – let's say because we've got 100 invoices over 30 days. Now, though, the management team can easily see the largest challenges we're facing, not just a one-off issue due to a lost invoice or holiday mail delays.

In the very real example of payments, we recognized the trend that many of our clients simply didn't use checks anymore. They are happy to pay, they just didn't have a way to pay.

The solution was simple: offer digital payments, offer automatic bill pay for annual services, and – with very few exceptions – stop accepting checks or using the mail for invoicing.

Can you create this system in your pest control business?

Of course. Here's a hint though: in the beginning, keep the information open ended. As you start to see problems and trends you need to address repeatedly, add more fields for information and data.

No matter what the error is, the goal is to understand why it happened. Then you and your team can make sure it doesn't happen again. This, too, is where your company's systems come into play. If you're depending on Randy to make his third stop before lunch, you're literally depending on Randy.

He might be a great guy; he might be the most efficient and experienced tech on your team.

But if Randy didn't sleep well last night, or he got in a fight with his wife, or you just "know" he can do three service calls before he takes lunch, you don't have a system, you just have Randy.

Do you think he's going to document himself?

Nope.

...But no matter how good or bad he is at his job, he's going to be open to sharing why he couldn't get to three calls before lunch IF there's a system that allows him to give you feedback. His first call was on the other side of town, the truck wasn't gassed up, his chemicals weren't restocked properly, or the homeowner was in the shower and didn't allow him to get begin the first service call until thirty minutes had passed since they didn't know Randy was coming that morning.

Do you see how simple this can be?

Do you understand how much feedback and data this can give you, no matter how robust your current systems are?

Do you see how this seamlessly integrates with Michael's management principles of innovation, quantification, and orchestration? More importantly, can you now see how this strategy gives you a clear line of sight into the systems and processes that aren't working?

The whole idea of an Error Log is to identify and make it easier to see recurring issues, and it points the way to where they came from. We absolutely keep track of not only where an error happens, but we look for trends in those errors too. A month with 200 scheduling errors and only 12 with first call resolution makes it pretty obvious what you and your team need to address. The more data you have, the easier it is to find patterns, and that's all the more reason to empower your team to share what they're seeing.

So here's the challenge you'll have to own: Ultimately, just like my story with Sarah, you're liable to find you're the cause of a lot of problems. Maybe not directly, but the training systems you've created, the hiring practices you've used, and even the materials and chemicals you purchase might all be points of failure in your Error Log and Accountability Board.

It works both ways, and if you truly want to "E-Myth" your business, you have to own ALL the results. There's no point in even finishing reading this book if you're not willing to admit mistakes and take action on them. If you will though, keep reading…

Fixing and Communicating

Good, you've kept reading! Let's talk about what to do with the information you've got…

First of all, if you can admit you don't have all the answers, it opens up TONS of ways to solve the challenges you and your team face in the pest control industry. Ultimately, to correct problems and fix issues, you'll need to have a system you and your team can follow to – you guessed it – fix broken systems.

You'll also need to be able to effectively communicate. Now the time for that is both before your take steps to correct the problem and after.

This is the core of how we are successful – communication. Information has to flow through any organization, both "up" and "down" and it is indispensable for handling change.

We do it through daily, weekly, monthly, and quarterly meetings, and while that may seem like a waste of time, I assure you, it isn't. A daily meeting isn't hours and hours of endless chatter, it's five minutes with a handful of employees.

Managers ask three simple questions:
- What's Up?

- How are we trending?
- Is anyone stuck?

Those three questions give us a quick snapshot of where our people are, where our metrics are, and if there is anything preventing our people from doing their job.

What more do you really need to get the day moving?

Of course, our weekly, monthly, and quarterly meetings are more robust, but even quarterly, the actual meeting time is only about 90 minutes.

It's just as important for me to mention here this isn't the only communications we have with our teams, especially in terms of their own satisfaction. While many companies – ourselves included – perform exit interviews to understand why people choose to leave, we also conduct "stay" interviews. You guessed it – to understand why people are staying.

Another key communication tool we use is questions focusing on "Start, Stop, or Keep." The idea, of course, is to find out what our people want us to … start, stop, or keep doing. The feedback our teams give us in these short conversations really brings new ideas, and bad ones, too, to our attention. After all, how many times have you found yourself in the field NOT following the systems you created? By asking and obtaining the feedback on what is working and what isn't, we're able to refine systems we would never know needed attention.

The point of all this communication is simple: it gives us the feedback we need as managers to identify the systems and processes we need. More importantly, it allows us to manage our business, not our people. ✤

On the Subject of Employees

Michael E. Gerber

*When you innovate, you've got to be prepared for people telling you
that you are nuts.*

—Larry Ellison, founder of Oracle Corporation

E very pest control contractor I've ever met has complained
about people.

About employees: "They come in late, they go home
early, they have the consistency of an antique boiler!"

About property managers: "They're living in a nonparallel
universe!"

About customers: "They think pesticides last six months!"

People, people, people. Every contractor's nemesis. And at the
heart of it all are the people who work for you.

"By the time I tell them how to do it, I could have done it twenty
times myself!" "How come nobody listens to what I say?" "Why is it
nobody ever does what I ask them to do?"

Does this sound like you?

So what's the problem with people? To answer that, think back to the last time you walked into a pest control business' office. What did you see in the employee's faces?

Most people working in pest control are harried. You can see it in their expressions. They're negative. They're tired. They're humorless. And with good reason! After all, they're surrounded by people who have roaches, damp crawlspaces, or—worst-case scenario—poisonous snakes, scorpions, or rodent infestations! Customers are looking for the most value for the least amount of money. And many are either angry or frightened. They don't want any problems with their homes.

Is it any wonder employees at most pest control businesses are disgruntled? They're surrounded by unhappy people all day. They're answering the same questions 24/7. And most of the time, the owner has no time for them. He or she is too busy leading a dysfunctional life.

Working with people brings great joy—and monumental frustration. And so it is with owners and their employees. But why? And what can we do about it?

Let's look at the typical pest control contractor —who this person is and isn't.

Most contractors are unprepared to use other people to get results. Not because they can't find people, but because they are fixated on getting the results themselves. In other words, most contractors are not the businesspeople they need to be, but *technicians suffering from an entrepreneurial seizure.*

Am I talking about you? What were you doing before you became an entrepreneur?

Were you a pest control technician working for a large commercial contractor? A subcontractor handling specific properties in a major metropolitan area? Or just doing odd jobs here and there?

Didn't you imagine owning your own business as the way out?

Didn't you think that because you knew how to do the technical work—because you knew so much about pesticide application and entomology—that you were automatically prepared to create a business that does that type of work?

Didn't you figure that by creating your own business you could dump the boss once and for all? How else to get rid of that impossible person, the one driving you crazy, the one who never let you do your own thing, the one who was the main reason you decided to take the leap into a business of your own in the first place?

Didn't you start your own business so that you could become your own boss?

And didn't you imagine that once you became your own boss, you would be free to do whatever you wanted to do—and to take home *all* the money?

Honestly, isn't that what you imagined? So you went into business for yourself and immediately dived into the work.

Doing it, doing it, doing it.

Busy, busy, busy.

Until one day you realized (or maybe not) that you were doing *all* of the work. You were doing everything you knew how to do, plus a lot more you knew nothing about. Building sweat equity, you thought.

In reality, a pest control technician suffering from an entrepreneurial seizure.

You were just hoping to make a buck in your own business. And sometimes you did earn a wage. But other times you didn't. You were the one signing the checks, all right, but they went to other people.

The bank that financed your truck.

The company you bought chemicals from.

The bookkeeper you had to hire.

The website or marketing company who built your website.

Everybody but, it seems, YOU!

Does this sound familiar? Is it driving you crazy?

Well, relax, because we're going to show you the right way to do it this time.

Read carefully. Be mindful of the moment. You are about to learn the secret you've been waiting for all your working life.

The People Law

It's critical to know this about the working life of contractors who own their own pest control business: *Without people, you don't own a company, you own a job.* And it can be the worst job in the world because you're working for a lunatic! (Nothing personal—but we've got to face facts.)

Let me state what every contractor knows: Without employees, you're going to have to do it all yourself. Without human help, you're doomed to try to do too much. This isn't a breakthrough idea, but it's amazing how many pest control business owners ignore the truth. They end up knocking themselves out, ten to twelve hours a day. They try to do more, but less actually gets done.

The load can double you over and leave you panting. In addition to the work you're used to doing, you may also have to do the books. And the organizing. And the filing. You'll have to do the planning and the scheduling. When you own your own business, the daily minutiae are never-ceasing—as I'm sure you've found out. Like painting the Golden Gate Bridge, it's endless. Which puts it beyond the realm of human possibility. Until you discover how to get it done by somebody else, it will continue on and on until you're a burned-out husk.

But with others helping you, things will start to drastically improve. If, that is, you truly understand how to engage people in the work you need them to do. When you learn how to do that, when you learn how to replace yourself with other people—employees trained in your system—then your business can really begin to grow. Only then will you begin to experience true freedom yourself.

What typically happens is that contractors, knowing they need help answering the phone, filing, and so on, go out and find people who can do these things. Once they delegate these duties, however, they rarely spend any time with the hoi polloi. Deep down, they feel it's not important *how* these things get done; it's only important that they get done.

They fail to grasp the requirement for a system that makes employees their greatest asset rather than their greatest liability. A system so reliable that if Chris dropped dead tomorrow, Leslie could do exactly what Chris did. That's where the People Law comes in.

The People Law says that each time you add a new person to your business using an intelligent (turnkey) system that works, you expand your reach. And you can expand your reach almost infinitely! People allow you to be everywhere you want to be simultaneously, without actually having to be there in the flesh.

Employees are to a pest control contractor what a record was to Frank Sinatra. A Sinatra record could be (and still is) played in a million places at the same time, regardless of where Frank was. And every record sale produced royalties for Sinatra (or his estate).

With the help of other people, Sinatra created a quality recording that faithfully replicated his unique talents, then made sure it was marketed and distributed, and the revenue managed.

Your employees can do the same thing for you. All *you* need to do is to create a "recording"—a system—of your unique talents, your special way of onboarding and servicing pest control, and then replicate it, market it, distribute it, and manage the revenue.

Isn't that what successful businesspeople do? Make a "recording" of their most effective ways of doing business? In this way, they provide a turnkey solution to their customers' problems. A system solution that really works.

Doesn't your business offer the same potential for you that records did for Sinatra (and now for his heirs)? The ability to produce income without having to go to work every day?

Isn't that what your employees could be for you? The means by which your system for sorting and servicing pest control could be faithfully replicated?

But first you've got to have a system. You have to create a unique way of doing business that you can teach to your employees, that you can manage faithfully, and that you can replicate consistently, just like McDonald's.

Because without such a system, without such a "recording," without a unique way of doing business that really works, all you're left with is people doing their own thing. And that is almost always a recipe for chaos. Rather than guaranteeing consistency, it encourages mistake after mistake after mistake.

And isn't that how the problem started in the first place? Employees doing whatever they perceived *they* needed to do, regardless of what you wanted? Employees left to their own devices, with no regard for the costs of their behavior? The costs to you?

In other words, employees without a system.

Can you imagine what would have happened to Frank Sinatra if he had followed that example? If every one of his recordings had been done differently? Imagine a million different versions of "My Way." It's unthinkable.

Would you buy a record like that? What if Frank was having a bad day? What if he had a sore throat?

Please hear this: The People Law is unforgiving. Without a systematic way of doing business, people are more often a liability than an asset. Unless you prepare, you'll find out too late which ones are which.

The People Law says that without a specific system for doing business; without a specific system for recruiting, hiring, and training your employees to use that system; and without a specific system for managing and improving your systems, your business will always be a crapshoot.

Do you want to roll the dice with your business at stake? Unfortunately, that is what most contractors are doing.

The People Law also says that you can't effectively delegate your responsibilities unless you have something specific to delegate. And that something specific is a way of doing business that works!

Frank Sinatra is gone, but his voice lives on. And someone is still counting his royalties. That's because Sinatra had a system that worked.

Now we will move on to the subject of *culture*. But before we do, let's see what Austin has to say about *employees*. ✤

Your People Are the Problem?

Austin Clark

"You, and the people around you, have to come up with all the rest of what it takes to build and run an organization."

—Brad and Geoff Smart, Topgrading

S ome of you might be taken aback by the title of this chapter, and that's not an accident. Your business, just like mine, is built around people. They work for you, they buy from you, and, yes, you are a person, too.

It might feel like I'm taking a step back in this chapter, but I assure you, it's right where it needs to be. We've discussed money, we've discussed management, and – to an extent – those subjects have touched on people.

However, here I need to push a few of your buttons.

Your people are human beings.

They have challenges – ex-spouses, elderly parents, young kids, house payments, car notes, hobbies, side gigs, and dozens of other things that *aren't* your business. That's not to say they don't like working for you, or they're mean, or they're dishonest, but their name, in most cases, isn't on the bottom line.

They don't sign the paychecks, they *earn* them.

Their passion and drive don't go far past their paycheck. Obviously, I believe this, and my own actions back up that belief – I put my wife's car in hock to make sure I could pay my team!

A business owner might be "okay" with losing money, but no employee ever is.

The fatal flaw for many pest control owners is this: they fail to recognize that their employees are just that - *employees*. When a growing pest control company begins to hire their first "real" teams, virtually all of them make the same mistakes I did – and it nearly cost me everything.

My own growth as an entrepreneur over the last two decades has made two things abundantly clear to me when it comes to people:

- Not everyone is cut out for growth.
- Skills and experience are no match for passion and integrity.

Let's talk about those separately, because while they have some of the same solutions, these are really two different challenges.

Not Everyone Is Cut Out For Growth

The point of this book is to show you how to grow your pest control business. Period. There's a hard lesson in that growth, though. Most, if not all, of the people in your company aren't prepared to make that journey with you. Facebook's sixth employee?

They don't work for Facebook anymore.

The same with Google.

The same with Uber, and Tik Tok, and any other company that has experienced truly incredible growth. The reason is simple – the company outgrew *them*. Now, that's not to say they're bad people, or they got fired, or anything derogatory about the situation, but your pest control business, when you do the things Michael and

I are telling you to do, is going to change. This time next year, it should not look like it does today.

The same for the year after that.

By now, you know I don't like to lose great people, but I temper that with the knowledge that I'm not serving my company – and my employees – by allowing them to stay in a position that's wrong for them. Are you doing that? Think of it this way – your employees are looking for stability in their jobs. Most, if not all, don't like a lot of change. Some of your longest-serving team members no doubt talk about "the good old days" when they could simply show up, spray a house, and leave an invoice or collect a check, then go on to the next house.

They like working in a *small* pest control business. Simple as that. When your growth means you need a field supervisor, or a new layer of management, those same long-term employees are not going to like it. They'll push back, they'll take longer to learn the system, or they may quit outright.

Verne Harnish touches on some of this in his book *Scaling Up*, and many other leaders have acknowledged the fact that the people who get you to certain milestones of growth - $500,000, $1 million, and beyond are very likely to not be able to continue with you as the growth accelerates.

It's not personal, it's just not the company they want to work for.

You need to come to grips with it, too; it's those goals and plans we discussed a few chapters ago. Can you evolve from a technician who built himself a job in pest control into the CEO of a pest control business that generates eight or nine figures in sales annually? The fact you're reading this book tells me you can, but you HAVE to be aware this book is not about your first technician Sam and his life. It's about you. Your life. Your growth as a person and an entrepreneur.

Sam has to work on himself, and he – like Facebook employee number six, might not be willing to come along for the journey you're on.

Skills and Experience Are No Match for Passion and Integrity

When I first began in the pest control industry, I took an incredibly competitive approach with our growth strategy that many in the industry feel is too costly and somewhat aggressive. Of course, I had been successful with it in the past, and I felt that my own passion would simply "will" it into a large-scale sales model.

Fortunately and unfortunately, as you'll see, the effort and investment I made allowed us to grow quickly and capture market share quickly.

Since I'd always loved to sell, I dug into our client acquisition and client fulfillment processes, and for me personally, it meant eighteen hour days and seemingly endless training and conversations with new and long-term customers. Within only a few months, the hard work began to pay off, and the Phoenix market - our home turf – grew to a million-dollar plus revenue stream.

It was working!

As a result, I (wrongly) rationalized that if I could build our entire team around that model, scaling and growth would simply be a matter of multiplying by "X." If a team of "X" size generated "X" profit, then a team of 5X would result in 5X profits.

Imagine what 10X could do!

I reached out to experienced people I knew from all facets of the home services industry and others I'd known in management and built a team to handle this expansion, and the money simply *rolled* in. The new teams were selling like crazy, the field teams were hitting the targets my data suggested they could, the managers were following the training I'd given them. Believe it or not, I didn't forget that I had a responsibility to the company, I dug in and began building training and mentoring programs to keep up with this new model.

You're probably nodding your head, knowing what happened next: systems started to fail during this growth frenzy. Systems I never thought would be tested began to collapse. Processes I didn't even think we'd need were suddenly needed.

...And up until that point, our growth had relied upon "experienced" people with high skill levels in specific areas.

I also made the near-fatal assumption that highly skilled and experienced people must surely share the passion I had for the work and the growth and the levels of integrity I brought to work each day. With so many new faces, and such dynamic growth, our reliance on passionate and highly skilled people to make conscious decisions in the absence of a system that supported them began to fall apart. You see, the processes required to scale to the million dollar mark tend to break - or are insufficient - at three million, five million, or ten million dollars.

I was forced to make a decision: slow our growth and potentially commit financial suicide or turn a blind eye to the problems.

...And while you might not have found yourself in that exact situation, I can guarantee you've been in one like it.

A lack of systems and oversight has allowed an employee to take advantage of the company or its clients, or maybe a poorly documented process creates a "net zero" or financial loss on every job.

Believe me, you're not alone. Ask ten owners of ten different pest control companies about their own growth and you'll find many of the same stories.

In my case, it was my own lack of understanding how to scale.

In yours, it might be the geographic range your business can reliably serve.

In another, it might be an office manager who is playing fast and loose with company funds.

It all boils down to the same core issues: Owners and leaders not understanding their own responsibilities. We might not like to admit it, but make no mistake, it IS why this happens.

The Aftermath

So, what actions did I take when I recognized my team wasn't adhering to our core values?

Simple: I didn't have jobs for them any more.

In so doing, our actions proved how important our mission statement and core values are to us as a company, and this was a visual reinforcement of that to our team. Heavy handed? Maybe.

Let me ask you though, where would you draw the line in sand if you caught an employee stealing?

$1? $10? $1,000? Theft often "feels" easier to define since you can place a definite dollar value on, but what about an employee who is rude to a customer?

What's the lifetime value of a *satisfied* customer in your business, versus one who simply is too complacent to cancel your services?

The reality was, by not upholding our core values and mission statement, those folks were doing our customers and our company an even larger disservice.

Since it's so critical, let me share our mission statement with you…

"To improve the quality of life for our customers, team, and community."

It's not really about pest control; pest control is simply the means to the end. *People* are what we're about. When we keep our mission about them, we can eliminate the bad apple mindset that allows someone to put profit over people. When you choose to lead with purpose instead of simply the services you offer, there's never any questions about what you and the company care about and how you will conduct your business.

Am I telling you anything you don't already know, as an owner in the pest control business?

Not at all.

The truth is, most of the difficult things in our lives are really simple, but we choose – for any variety of reasons – to make them hard.

If you want to lose weight, that's simple: don't eat as many calories as you burn each day.

If you want to make more money in your business, that's simple too: charge more for the same services or create a way to get more clients.

Many times, we get caught in the trap of "needing more information." We've all heard the phrase, "Knowledge is power," and with the sheer amount of data and information we have access to today, we can get lost in the analysis of a tactic or idea while never actually doing anything about a problem.

You've got one employee right now - I'll virtually guarantee – that you think you can't live without.

Depending on the size of your pest control business, it could be a technician, but it's likely someone who handles things in your office, and they make life hard for you.

You're making excuses about why you tolerate their actions, or their attitudes, or the nearly constant management they need. I've seen it time and again – an office manager who refuses to make decisions, bookkeepers who don't follow any sort of logic in keeping those books, and technicians who are slow, rude, and sloppy in their execution.

And yet, there you are, making excuses to yourself and your partners, "We can't do it without Jim." Or Jill. Or Jack. Or *whoever…*

Let me tell you right now, the rest of your team knows, and they hate it. They see it as a weakness, or as preferential treatment, and it isn't helping your morale at the same time it costs you time and money.

You've got the choice – continue the constant management of that individual, or create the systems, processes, and solutions in your business that will solve those challenges.

Does that mean firing them? Maybe. But it could also mean addressing the problem areas directly or indirectly to allow them to meet the standards you've set. In reality, if you simply terminate them, you really haven't solved the problem that exists, you simply solved a *symptom* of the problem. Your next hire may or may not give you that same challenge, but guess what?

The opportunity for it to happen again still exists.

It's far better to take the time to address *why* you've got the problem in the first place and solve it than to be constantly riding the merry-go-round of hiring and training people only to have them leave. It's the culmination of the various plans we talked about a few chapters ago.

It's the Operations Manual of your business. It doesn't matter if it's a physical binder, a digital website, or a series of PDFs, it answers everything.

"This is the step-by-step system we use for all new contracts, page 15."

"This is how we answer the phone at all times, page 43."

"This is the process for completing our first treatment at a new client's home, pages 32-36."

Ultimately, when the owner of a pest control business makes the decision to delegate – and let's be honest, that first new hire is almost ALWAYS an administrative or office assistant – they nearly always make three fatal mistakes:

- They create a basic list of what needs to be done, planning on hiring an "experienced" person to fill in those blanks based on how the job was done somewhere else.
- They believe that list is set in stone and never needs to be updated, adjusted, or managed.
- They abdicate their responsibility to that aspect of their business because they think it's "taken care of."

If you have any plans to grow your pest control business, the only way is through delegation. You'll need a team, and that team will need guidance. Not the guidance many of us received as we were learning the industry – an experienced technician telling us how to do the job while we were on the job with him, but a replicable, written, logical system that takes them, step by step, through every part of the job they are hired to do.

When you accept the responsibility to begin to think and act like an entrepreneur instead of a technician, you need to be comfortable with the idea that every system is a work in progress. More importantly, that every system can and should be open to innovation. The right people will share some of that burden with you, but you can't expect them to be the only ones. This is the real work of the pest control entrepreneur. ✤

CHAPTER

11

On the Subject of Culture

Michael E. Gerber

Meaningful relationships and meaningful work are mutually reinforcing, especially when supported by radical truth and radical transparency.

—Ray Dalio

If you're a sole practitioner—that is, you're selling only yourself—then your pest control company, called a sole proprietorship, will never make the leap to the pest control business called a company. The progression from sole proprietorship to business to enterprise demands that you hire other technicians to do what you do (or don't do). In some cases, these people might be subcontractors, but they might also be your very first employees.

Subcontractors are different from regular employees in all states. They operate under different laws and regulations as owners of their solely-owned company. No matter what name they operate under, they too, must operate within your System. To the degree they don't, you're in trouble.

As a pest control owner, whether your first "team" is made of subcontractors or simply "good" people, you now know (or should know) that "people" can be a huge problem. Until you face this special business problem, your sole proprietorship will never become a business, and your business will certainly never become an enterprise.

Solving the Hiring Problem

Let's say you're about to partner with a subcontractor or hire your first employee. Certainly, this is someone who has specific skills within the pest control industry: maybe they handle bedbugs, or rodents, or commercial work, whatever. It all starts with choosing the right personnel. After all, these are the people to whom you are delegating your responsibility and for whose behavior you are completely liable. Remember Frank Sinatra? Do you really want to leave that choice to chance? Are you that much of a gambler? I hope not.

If you've never hired before, how do you really know he or she is skilled? For that matter, what does "skilled" mean?

For you to make an intelligent decision about this person, you must have a working definition of the word *skilled*. Your challenge is to know *exactly* what your expectations are, then to make sure your other employees or subcontractors operate with precisely the same expectations. Failure here almost assures a breakdown in your relationship.

I want you to write the following on a piece of paper: "By *skilled*, I mean ..." Once you create your personal definition, it will become a standard for you and your business, for your customers, and for your employees and subcontractors.

A standard, according to *Webster's Eleventh*, is something "set up and established by authority as a rule for the measure of quantity, weight, extent, value, or quality."

Thus, your goal is to establish a measure of quality control, a standard of skill, which you will apply to everyone you hire or contract with. More important, you are also setting a standard for the performance of your company.

By creating standards for your selection—standards of skill, performance, integrity, financial stability, and experience—you have begun the powerful process of building a culture *and* a company that can operate exactly as you expect it to.

By carefully thinking about exactly what to expect, you have already begun to improve your business.

In this enlightened state, you will see the hiring and selection process as an opportunity to define what you (1) intend to provide for your customers, (2) expect from your employees, and (3) demand for your life.

Powerful stuff, isn't it? Are you up to it? Are you ready to feel your rising power?

Don't rest on your laurels just yet. Defining those standards is only the first step you need to take. The second step is to create a *Personnel Development System.*

A Personnel Development System is an action plan designed to tell you what you are looking for in a team member – or a subcontractor. It includes the exact benchmarks, accountabilities, timing of fulfillment, and budget you will assign to the process of looking for employees and subcontractors, identifying them, recruiting them, interviewing them, training them, managing their work, auditing their performance, compensating them, reviewing them regularly, and terminating or rewarding them for their performance.

All of these things must be documented—actually *written down*— if they're going to make any difference to you, your technicians, your managers, or your bank account!

And then you've got to persist with that system, come hell or high water. Just as Ray Kroc did at Mc Donald's. Just as Walt Disney did at Disneyland. Just as Sam Walton did at Walmart.

This leads us to our next topic of discussion: the subject of *profits*. But first, let's read what Austin has to say on the subject of hiring. ✤

Building a Culture of Improvement

Austin Clark

"You cannot hope to build a better world without improving the individuals. To that end, each of us must work for his own improvement and, at the same time, share a general responsibility for all humanity, our particular duty being to aid those to whom we think we can be most useful."

—Marie Curie

It's no secret that *The E-Myth* is built upon a rock of systems and processes, and I can honestly say that the mistakes I made in our first efforts to grow weren't due to a lack of systems to conduct sales, but rather, a lack of systems and processes to ensure our company's mission was being carried out properly by our entire team.

Looking back, my heart was in the right place, but I had made some fatal assumptions.

At that time, I believed that highly skilled (and frankly, expensive) people – both hourly, salaried, and subcontractors - were the key to growth, and that a relatively simple system could manage those people. After all, they were professionals, right? How much hand-holding would I have to do? My mistake was assuming they cared as much about the business and the results as I did.

Here's the hard truth: I would have been far better off to hire a group of average people with integrity and a commitment to themselves and then create the systems and processes to train and develop the skills they need to succeed.

It would absolutely have been better than wondering if my team was going to do the right thing in the field.

The story of that version of our business and our early challenges with that business model are not so different as hundreds – or even thousands – of other pest control companies in the world. You've heard them, probably even experienced them; the incompetent office manager who doesn't have a clue; the old technician no one gets along with; the part-time marketing and social media subcontractor who never understood the work or the industry.

Our challenges were just another example.

How you choose to react to those challenges is what will – or won't – grow your company.

Nearly every pest control company that experiences something like I did does the same thing – they get small again. But then what? For me, it was a wake-up call that our core values and our mission truly were the most critical thing to me. For you, it might be something similar, or it could simply be your own dream that you can create a system that will finally allow you to safely exit the daily operations of your pest control company.

When I realized what was truly the most important thing, upholding our core values and mission, I could begin to build the systems we needed to support that. Until then, I had operated under the naïve belief that the answer to my company's growth was simple: just keep hiring skilled people and paying them well.

The thing I learned, and what Michael has said for decades, is that skilled people, or those with loads of experience, cost too much (which was certainly true) and often have ingrained habits that can't be easily broken (which was *definitely* true). Even worse?

They *know* how good they are, and how in demand their skills can be in many companies.

I'm not telling you highly skilled people are bad for your pest control company, but I am telling you, most of the actual work that needs to be done, the day-to-day, technical things, doesn't need an expert, it needs a well-built system.

Yes, find a *great* CPA.

Yes, find a *great* attorney.

Yes, find a *great* mentor.

…But if your bookkeeping is done in-house? Find a *good* book-keeper who can and will follow the systems and processes you and that great CPA deem appropriate for the business. Find an *average* technician who will operate with integrity and is a fundamentally good person - and then teach him or her a great system.

Find people who can follow direction and are teachable, and then teach them the systems you've created to allow them to do the job properly - every time.

Great systems show a normal person how to provide an extraordinary result.

It Began with Culture

For me, rebuilding began with a focus on our culture. I recognized its importance to our business, and our first systems revolved around hiring and training. We vowed to hire slow and fire fast, and we accepted that teaching good people a great system would take up time on the front end of their training but pay off big once that training was at least partially complete. I'll explain more about that in a few minutes…

Collectively, leadership agreed it would be better to be under-staffed than to have bad apples in the barrel with us, and that's what we did.

It was painful too. I watched as I lost so many of the big gains we had accomplished; I watched as new markets I had opened struggled; and, because of my analytical nature, I dug into metrics and began focusing on how we trained people – and what it really cost us.

There are a lot of ways of calculating the costs of a bad employee – the costs of acquiring them, any losses they are responsible for in terms of canceled customers, the lifetime value of that customer, and the actual time your team spent training that person.

I've seen data that suggests it's as low as thirty percent of their annual salary, and I've also seen it stated it's as much as THREE times their annual salary.

Any way you pitch that data, the wrong hire can cost you a lot of money.

This is where I started building from though. I began listening to clients: why they were leaving, how they viewed our organization, where we had not fulfilled our promises to them, and what they actually wanted.

This extended into services, billing, contracts, communication, and every other level of the business, and it gave me a place to start. This was the very beginning of the Error Log and the Accountability Board I shared with you a few chapters ago and was nearly two years in the making. The results of that hard work though, speak for themselves.

…And even though I've described what the Error Log is designed to do, it's important to realize it is really just one piece of a far bigger system. A system that allows our team – and the individuals who are a part of it – to improve every day. Those daily, weekly, monthly, and quarterly meetings I talked about earlier?

Those are the opportunities for managers to get real-time feedback about what's going on – not only in our systems, but with our people. The idea though, is to not only get the data, but also, to foster the relationships with our teams to keep communication flowing daily. As I've tracked it, it's become clear to me this has allowed us to grow faster and to quickly address issues long before they become challenges.

Today, I can honestly say that hiring with integrity to our core values and mission statement, and fostering an environment with great training and feedback systems, has been the single biggest factor in our success.

From those daily meetings, each team member sits down once a week with their manager to discuss anything on the Error Log. This meeting might only be five to ten minutes, and it's not about beating up an employee about a mistake, it's about bringing those mistakes into the conversation so they don't happen again.

They could make the same error 100 times in a week, but the expectation isn't to lambast them over it, it's to make sure they lower that number the next week.

Make it 99 times, and show that you're learning.

When it comes to monthly meetings, you guessed it: we have a replicable system to rank and score every part of our operation. These are all-day affairs for the management team, and in eight hours, you'd be shocked at the volume of work that can be done. If you're looking to improve the management team and systems in your own pest control business, my experience has shown it's best to pick the top two or three areas where you can prove your company is weakest and go to work there.

When you address this low-hanging fruit, you can often move the needle in your own business quickly and make big gains.

Trust me, if you aren't talking about something to your team and your managers, they aren't focusing on it - even if you think it should be obvious. That's where the idea of monthly scorecards came in, to help us identify areas of weakness and improve transparency and accountability.

The idea is simple: every employee has a scorecard with their name, the month, and a grade of A, B, or C. Every month, they'll focus on eight to twelve outcomes they want to have, and then, in the monthly scorecard review, we go over their progress.

This has two specific benefits. First, we can look at the goals and outcomes to see if they were met. Secondly though, when an outcome is met, we can see how that was done. As a result, we might just discover a new – or better – way to do things as a company.

For the employee, if they have achieved the outcome, that's great for them, but if they've fallen short, they know it's something they need to improve. By doing this type of meeting monthly, employees are getting faster feedback and can grow and develop faster than they could in a business that only evaluates employees annually.

And you guessed it, there are far fewer surprises when it comes to turnover.

As a pest control business owner, I can already hear you, "Austin, even if I had the time, the sheer amount of work and money to execute this type of training and feedback is hard to fathom!"

Yes, it is. We spend thousands of dollars and hours every year simply doing these daily, weekly, monthly and quarterly meetings. I look at it as a proactive way of spending money and time we'd have to spend in other places if our training and feedback systems weren't so robust.

I'd be spending it to acquire new leads.

I'd be spending it to hire (more) new employees.

I'd be spending it handling dissatisfied clients.

I'd be spending it in undocumented conversations with team members with an idea or a problem.

When you and I woke up this morning, we had – and still do – the same number of seconds in our day. How we choose to spend those seconds, and the overall impact those seconds will have on our business over time, will be the deciding factor in our success.

You can keep fixing the same problem over and over, or you can face it head on and develop a solution to it so you can continue to grow.

It's critical you recognize that all these systems, all these meetings, and all this feedback aren't developed to micromanage people, but rather, to set them free to be themselves.

Our systems don't require salespeople to "hard sell" potential customers, and our processes don't force our technicians to have to worry about how to act when they are in a client's home. It's right there, in black and white: each process, each system, each step. Not only will we show them how to do the job, we engage with them every day to make sure they don't have problems.

Perhaps some of you might take exception to this idea that by systemizing so much, and concentrating on "good" people, we're somehow dehumanizing them, or turning them into robots. Nothing could be farther from the truth.

What we've done is allow them not to have to approach every task, or sale, or job with any kind of trepidation. By no longer having to worry about how to do something, or what's "right" or "wrong," they can now concentrate on simply doing it. To put it another way, let's look at it like this…

- With a uniform policy, they aren't wondering what to wear.
- With a process for selling our services, they aren't struggling to make a sale.
- With a system to follow for all treatments in a customer's home, they know exactly what to do and when to do it.
- With a policy for how to check out, stock, fuel, and maintain a truck in our fleet, they know exactly what should be on the truck at all times, how much product is to be kept in it, and when it needs to be washed.

In other words, the system runs the business and our people run the system!

Contrast that with some of the challenges and worries a team without those systems and processes in place has, and tell me who gets the better deal?

The result is what I call a Culture of Improvement. We find and hire people with the proper characteristics to honor our core values and mission, then we give them systems that allow them to be supported. Month after month, this allows them to improve themselves, both professionally and personally.

So, What About Those Values?

I already shared our Mission - "*To improve the quality of life for our customers, team, and community*" – so let me share those Core Values also.

- Do the Right Thing
- Be Nice
- Be the Solution
- Keep Improving

Here's the thing: Not ONE of these has anything to do with pest control. Sure, we could easily staff our entire team with "experienced" people from the industry, and many of them might be perfect in terms of their own commitment to our values.

If, as an entrepreneur, you'll actually take the time to create the systems and processes your company needs, you'll find the number of highly qualified people that are happy to be a part of a team is far greater than you ever imagined.

It takes work, certainly, but the results are worth it.

Our systems free our team from having to rely on "experience" and that allows them to take on and continue to learn more about their job, their industry, and, more importantly, themselves.

It's important to recognize, these are the values of my company. To a degree, they are also my personal values, and they show in the company I've helped to build. But as good as your training systems can be, they can't make a tiger change their stripes. Our training programs can't make people into something they aren't disposed to be. I can't make a mean person "be nice." I can't make an unhappy or bland person into a champion of customer service with a bubbly personality on the phone.

So while I counsel you to not hire "experienced" or "highly skilled" people, and Michael has long taught to create systems and processes to allow normal people to do extraordinary things, make no mistake – my "normal" person still has a true heart of gold.

As Michael has said, "every small business is a school," and I can think of no better way to serve people than to help them to grow. By changing our focus from finding "good" people – meaning those with loads of experience and high skills levels – to finding *better* people, with integrity, a desire to learn, and the ability to help us document and solve challenges, our ability to scale, to expand, and to develop systems that support our operation has been far better than I ever thought possible. ✤

On the Subject of Estimates

Michael E. Gerber

You can't manage what you can't measure.

—Peter Drucker

One of the greatest weaknesses of pest control companies is accurately estimating how long jobs will take and then scheduling their customers accordingly. *Webster's Collegiate Dictionary* defines estimate as "a rough or approximate calculation." Anyone who has worked on a jobsite knows that those estimates can be rough indeed.

Do you want to see someone who gives you a rough approximation? What if your doctor gave you a rough approximation of your medical condition?

The fact is, we can predict many things we don't typically predict. For example, there are ways to calculate for common problems. Look at the steps of the process. Most of the things you do are standard, so develop a step-by-step system and stick to it.

In my book *The E-Myth Manager*, I raised eyebrows by suggesting that doctors eliminate the waiting room. Why? You don't need it if you're always on time. The same goes for a pest control company. If you're always on time, then your customers don't have to wait.

What if the owner of a pest control company made this promise: on time, every time, as promised, or we pay for it.

"Impossible!" contractors cry. "Each job is different. We simply can't know how long each will take."

Do you follow this? Since these owners believe they're incapable of knowing how to organize their time, they build a business based on lack of knowing and lack of control. They build a business based on estimates.

I once had a contractor ask me, "What happens when we discover a customer has an infestation we didn't know about? How can we deal with something so unexpected? How can we give proper service and stay on schedule?"

My first thought was that it's not being dealt with now. Few contractors are able to give generously of their time. Ask anyone who's been to a contractor's office lately. It's chaos.

The solution is interest, attention, analysis. Try detailing what you do at the beginning of a job, what you do in the middle, and what you do at the end. How long does each take? In the absence of such detailed, quantified standards, everything ends up being an estimate, and a poor estimate at that.

However, a pest control business organized around a system has time for proper attention. It's built right into the system.

Too many contractors have grown accustomed to thinking in terms of estimates without thinking about what the term really means. Is it any wonder many pest control businesses are in trouble?

Enlightened pest control owners, in contrast, banish the word *estimate* from their vocabulary. When it comes to estimating, just say no!

"But you can never be exact," contractors have told me for years. "Close, maybe. But never exact."

I have a simple answer to that: *You have to be.* You simply can't afford to be inexact. You can't accept inexactness in yourself or in your pest control business.

You can't go to work every day believing that your business, the work you do, and the commitments you make are all too complex and unpredictable to be exact. With a mindset like that, you're doomed to run a sloppy ship. A ship that will eventually sink and suck you down with it!

This is so easy to avoid. Sloppiness—in both thought and action—is the root cause of your frustrations.

The solution to those frustrations is clarity. Clarity gives you the ability to set a clear direction, which fuels the momentum you need to grow your business.

Clarity, direction, momentum—they all come from insisting on exactness.

But how do you create exactness in a hopelessly inexact world? The answer is this. You discover the exactness in your business by refusing to do any work that can't be controlled exactly.

The only other option is to analyze the market, determine where the opportunities are, and then organize your business to be the exact provider of the services you've chosen to offer.

Two choices, and only two choices: (1) Evaluate your business and then limit yourself to the tasks you know you can do exactly, or (2) start all over by analyzing the market, identifying the key opportunities in that market, and building a business that operates exactly.

What you cannot do, what you must refuse to do, from this day forward, is to allow yourself to operate with an inexact mindset. It will lead you to ruin.

Which leads us inexorably back to the word I have been using through this book: *systems.*

Who makes estimates? Only contractors who are unclear about exactly how to do the task in question. Only contractors whose experience has taught them that if something can go wrong, it will—and to them!

I'm not suggesting that a systems solution will guarantee that you always perform exactly as promised. But I am saying that a systems solution will faithfully alert you when you're going off track, and will do it before you have to pay the price for it.

In short, with a systems solution in place, your need to estimate will be a thing of the past, both because you have organized your business to anticipate mistakes, and because you have put into place the system to do something about those mistakes before they blow up.

There's this, too: To make a promise you intend to keep places a burden on you and your site supervisors to dig deeply into how you intend to keep it. Such a burden will transform your intentions and increase your attention to detail.

With the promise will come dedication. With dedication will come integrity. With integrity will come consistency. With consistency will come results you can count on. And results you can count on mean that you get exactly what you hoped for at the outset of your business: the true pride of ownership that every contractor should experience.

This brings us to the subject of *customers*. Who are they? Why do they come to you? How can you identify yours? And who *should* your customers be? But first let's listen to what Austin has to say about *estimating*. ✤

C H A P T E R

14

Revenue is Vanity and Profit is Sanity

Austin Clark

"Profit or loss is not guaranteed. That depends on the consumer and depends on the product. That's a risk that business people take."
—Mukesh Ambani

Your pest control business doesn't exist because of estimates, it exists between – and because of - two important groups – your suppliers and your clients. That spot isn't static either. It moves this way and that, depending on thousands of variables. The Covid pandemic that began in 2020 has not only shown us how easy it is to upset supply chains, but also how quickly any service company needs to react in order to stay in business.

The truth of it all is this: the difference between your business thriving and surviving typically comes down to one thing – the ability of you and your team to reliably calculate the costs involved with every job.

In other words, your pricing.

For many pest control companies, pricing – *not* estimating - is almost magical. Yes, it can be hard, but in reality, once you understand it, it's easy to become a real master of it. One key takeaway from my own experience: *don't try to do everything for everyone, everywhere.*

Chances are, you've tried that, just like I did, and it is extraordinarily frustrating. As I was really digging in and growing my business a decade or so ago, I wasn't really sure who we were, or who we might one day be, so I said yes to every job.

Every job.

With little or no thought to the actual costs and pricing of that job, or the profit it could generate.

I finally had my "ah-ha!" in, of all places, Paradise Valley.

A new customer had called us, asking for service, and even though I knew how far out of our usual service area (in those days) they were, I'd said yes. The demographics of the neighborhood were great, and I felt it would be a perfect opportunity to begin to grow our book of business in that area.

What I didn't account for in my "estimate" was the time.

More than an extra hour of driving, plus our regular services that would take nearly two hours, and we still only charged our normal rate.

Our estimate was ALL wrong, and for a lot of reasons.

When I agreed to the job, and didn't adjust the pricing, I single handedly put revenue over profitability. Just like the title of this chapter – revenue is simply vanity, and you can't pay the bills with vanity.

Ten million dollars in revenue is still a loss if your expenses are ten million dollars and one penny.

Simply put, you're losing money, and with no profit, there can be no reinvestment in the business, no more hiring, no more training, no new technology, and no more marketing.

A dead business, in other words.

Now, I know what you're thinking, so let me stop you right there.

"Austin, my accountant told me to manage down my deductions and expenses as close to zero as I can to limit my taxes! How is that wrong?"

I'm not going to go so far as to throw rocks at a CPA, or to even give you tax advice, but the truth is that if you actively manage your profits *down*, you aren't focused on them.

You're focused on hitting a number, and before we get sidetracked by that ideology, let me simply say this: if you can't show profitability year after year, or you only show *enough* profitability year after year to minimize taxes, you're devaluing your business. Who wants to buy a business that is just barely squeaking by?

What bank wants to lend money to that business owner? That's not just in terms of a business loan, that's also for your home, and even business lines of credit.

If your company shows plenty of profit though, you don't have that problem. We pay a LOT of taxes annually, but we earn far more than enough not to have to worry about where that money is coming from.

Why?

It all goes back to understanding costs and eliminating estimates. And embracing *pricing*.

Since that moment of clarity in Paradise Valley, I realized how critical it was to ensure every job carried a significant amount of profit in it. It wasn't always an easy thing to sort out, but it's been extremely rewarding.

Reverse Engineering Your Prices

The first step to effectively understanding your pricing is getting clear about your costs. Specifically, your Cost of Goods Sold (COGS). EVERY pest control company has this, especially if you find yourself providing much of the day-to-day labor. Essentially, it's exactly what it sounds like – the cost to manufacture the good or service. Everything that goes into producing your goods and services. Chemicals, supplies, fuel, labor, uniforms, even, in some cases, the vehicles in your company. If you could only look at one line in your Profit and Loss statements, COGS is the one. (But it shouldn't be the only one you look at!)

Cost of Goods Sold is the leading indicator of what your net profit should be. Period.

If you don't have a clue about all of this, and simply depend on a bookkeeper and your CPA to magically do it all for you, you need to stop. You need to schedule time with them to understand what goes into your COGS, and how that relates to your net profit. When you really dig into your costs, you can begin to set yourself up for success in your pricing ... and your profits!

With a basic understanding of your costs, you can begin to reverse engineer everything else.

Ask yourself, "What is the profit margin I want left over each month?" It might be tempting to pick out a number that sounds good, but again, doing some research into your market and the competition can give you a clear idea of what people expect.

You don't have to be married to someone else's numbers though. If "everyone" else is charging $75 for a standard treatment, and you want to charge $95, go for it! Just understand how your company adds value to every client. It might be how you schedule; it might be how you collect payments; it might even be the fact you can treat on weekends.

In short, *any* price difference over the area average can be handled by marketing. Right now, let's simply get you the perfect price.

The basic formula is this: subtract your profit margin (in decimal form) from the number 1.

Let's say you want a 23% profit margin. That'd be 1 – 0.23. The answer is 0.77.

Now take your COGS and divide it by 0.77.

In a restaurant's example, if the cost of goods sold for a hamburger is $10, and you're aiming at a profit of 20%, you would take that $10 and divide it by 0.8 (1 minus that 20%). Your menu price for that burger is $12.50.

That represents the exact price you need to charge for your product or service to hit your goals. Obviously, you need to make sure to account for ALL the costs of your own "hamburger" or you'll struggle to hit your goals.

...But even though you have identified a price, it doesn't mean it's the only one.

Every service has a price, and therefore, you need to look at every service's pricing in this way. Then have the discipline to stick to your strategy. You cannot try to do everything for everyone because if you keep trying to do "one off" work, your cost of goods can easily skyrocket and send your profits tumbling.

To do that, we've got some more work to do...

Create a Core

As I took these same steps years ago, I made some hard decisions and collected some reliable data. I know what our pricing could be, but I also had to get incredibly clear on two factors that would affect what we actually did with that pricing. If you want your pest control company to grow and expand, you'll need to know these also.

- Who is my Ideal Customer?
- What is my best product or service?

In Michael's writing, this is the world of your Dream, Vision, Purpose, and Mission, but even if you're not a long-time student of The E-Myth Revisited (and you really *should* have read it), it all starts right here. When you allow yourself to focus on one specific type of customer and one or two very focused products, at least initially, you avoid being spread too thin.

You absolutely can expand, but until you dial in and sort the first one out, you can't effectively move to the next one. What you're going to realize is that this process is really no different than the way you approach building systems elsewhere in your pest control business. Here's the thing though, by recognizing who you serve and what you do, it's also incredibly empowering.

Now you know when to say "no."

You've effectively defined what you will and won't do, and how you'll do it ... and what you'll charge for that service.

This may sound strange, but it's often really hard for us, as entrepreneurs, to turn down a job. We can rationalize the business, and perhaps we figure that since it's an outlier, it's somehow more profitable, but it usually isn't.

Remember, every time you say "yes" to something that isn't aligned perfectly with your business, you're also saying "no" to something else – likely, something that IS more profitable, something that won't take as much time, and something that you know EXACTLY how to do.

Just because you *can* doesn't mean that you *should*. You must respect that there is only so much time in every day, and you only have so many resources to do the work. Establishing who you serve and how you serve them allows you to be confident in the choices you make. When you eliminate the distractions and stay true to your core focuses, you can be far more active in growing the products and services you are best at – and that provide the real profit you're looking for.

Understanding Price Increases

When you finally learn how to stick to your core business, and you develop the processes and systems that run those aspects of your business, inevitably, you'll be faced with expansion.

For me, simply having the confidence that our business model not only worked but was profitable allowed me to begin the first steps of expansion.

We began to look at potential clients outside of our traditional service area.

Remember that job in Paradise Valley? When I ran my COGS numbers on a job like that, I realized I should charge $250.

Not only was that what we began to offer, that was what we *sold*. In the long run, those increases are incremental, say, 2-5% every other year, but initially? We did have far larger increases, too, with data to back up our decisions and marketing in place to validate the higher rates.

...And that's just one example of when we charged more for our services.

You might be worried about having to discuss a price increase with a long-term customer; after all, who wants to pay more for a service, right?

Stop thinking like that.

Gasoline, groceries, healthcare, cars, attorneys – don't they all cost more now than they used to? I can well remember "the good old days" when we could buy a new service truck for $12,000. Today – less than two decades later – the equivalent version of that truck is just shy of $30,000! Not to mention employee wages, gas, chemicals and other materials are all following that same trend.

Just as importantly, think about businesses and services you use in your daily life – your Netflix account, gym, internet services, car insurance. How often do you get an email about those rates going up?

You haven't canceled them yet, have you?

Chances are, your clients aren't going to cancel you because you've raised your rates either. And even if they do (and I've seen this time and again), I can virtually guarantee they'll come back to you later.

...And pay the going rate when they do.

The key to this is providing value to your clients. They're generally happy to stay with you even through a price increase if you've taken the time to build a business relationship with them that allows them to see the value of that 2-5% price increase.

One of the key strategies we've implemented is to raise prices every other year. It's not about gouging people or making a killing off of them. It's about producing profits that allow us to reinvest into our business and continue to grow.

As a pest control business owner, it should be your goal to constantly improve the value of your products and services that you offer customers. In order to best do that, it may require you to raise prices.

The Pricing Conversation

The funny thing about most pest control owners – they're incredibly good at the technical work they do, but struggle with sales conversations. Of course, that sets up challenges in the very subjects we're talking about, from COGS, to saying "no," to discussing price increases.

As we've grown, I've seen dozens of examples of this sort of dereliction of duty from around the country: from clients who have never had their prices increased (for decades!), to clients who have relocated outside of regular service areas, but are still in the same metropolitan area, to keypunch errors that weren't caught and allowed customers to lock in one-time discounts for years at a time.

How do you navigate that conversation … without making them upset?

Well, for starters, you have to recognize *you're not wrong*. The services and prices you charge are arrived at through a logical, methodical system, and thus, aren't negotiable. At the same time, the customer isn't "wrong" or "bad" for not wanting to pay more – we're humans.

Step one is simple – don't take it personally, it's just business.

The next step, and the one that really has made the difference for us, is communication.

We do it as many ways as we possibly can, and we'll use the medium our clients want us to use.

If they like email, we'll send email. If they like text, we'll send a text. Phone call? Our teams can ring them right up. And yes, if they want to use the regular mail and get a letter, no problem. We'll do that too.

Another key to the communication is transparency. We don't sugar-coat things and we don't beat around the bush. If there's a difficult message to deliver – a price increase, in this case – then we simply state the facts … and there are more facts to a price increase than simply stating you're raising their rates on September 1st.

We'll share the benefits they're getting from their relationship with us – automated bill pay, or our simple scheduling, for example. We'll also explain how we have improved in the previous two years and share how their investment is paying off in a higher quality service.

It's NEVER just about a price increase; it's about a *service* increase, and it's ALL about communication.

There's a Price to Confidence

The truth is, many pest control company owners are technicians, and conversations about sales and pricing – and the very non-technical work of arriving at realistic prices – represents something we're not always comfortable doing.

This comes right back to one of the most important things you need as an entrepreneur in the pest control business: confidence. Now, if you're worried about the overall quality of your operation and the service you provide?

You guessed it, a price increase can be a painful conversation to have. If that's the case, though, the solution is simple: take the ideas Michael and I are sharing and implement them! *Earn* that price increase!

You have to be confident NOT just in the work you do, but in the processes that support your work. Let me share something that surprised me when I began doing the true work of the entrepreneur – one of the top three sources for new clients is actually returning clients.

People who knew us, left us, and now have come back.

It might be because they realized we really are "that" good, or they've come to understand the competition isn't as good as they said they were. They might even have left because we did raise prices.

Any way you look at it, they came back, and we have the data to prove it.

Returning clients are great, and what's so amazing to me is they *have* come back. They've tried the alternatives and been let down, and when they come back, they come back at the higher rate, with no complaints and stay forever.

So, as we close this chapter, let me leave you with this piece of advice...

Have the confidence in yourself and the work you do – both the tactical and strategic – to create a pricing structure that drives the profits you want to see in your pest control company.

If a client chooses to leave, don't try to lower your prices to make a bad deal "work." Don't lower YOUR standards to capture revenues, keep them high so you can capture *profits*. Remind your clients of the value you've built into your systems and processes, and if they choose to leave, be gracious to them, because if you run your company the way you should, they'll be back ... and they'll gladly pay the prices that were "too high" before! ✤

On the Subject of Customers

Michael E. Gerber

Whether individuals or organizations, we follow those who lead not because we have to, but because we want to. We follow those who lead not for them, but for ourselves.

—Simon Sinek

When it comes to the business of pest control, the best definition of customers I've ever heard is this:

Customers: very special people who drive most owners crazy.

Does that work for you?

After all, it's a rare customer who shows any appreciation for what a pest control company has to go through to do the job as promised. Don't they always think the price is too high? And don't they focus on problems, broken promises, and the mistakes they think you make, rather than all the ways you bend over backward to give them what they need?

Do you ever hear other owners in the industry voice these complaints? More to the point, have you ever voiced them yourself? Well, you're not alone. I have yet to meet a pest control contractor who doesn't suffer from a strong case of customer confusion.

Customer confusion is about:

- What your customer really wants
- How to communicate effectively with your customer
- How to keep your customer truly happy
- How to deal with customer dissatisfaction
- Whom to call a customer

Confusion 1: What Your Customer Really Wants

Your customers aren't just people; they're very specific kinds of people. Let me share with you the six categories of customers as seen from the E-Myth marketing perspective: (1) tactile customers, (2) neutral customers, (3) withdrawal customers, (4) experimental customers, (5) transitional customers, and (6) traditional customers.

Your entire marketing strategy must be based on which type of customer you are dealing with. Each of the six customer types spends money on pest control services for very different, and identifiable, reasons. These are:

- Tactile customers get their major gratification from interacting with other people.
- Neutral customers get their major gratification from interacting with inanimate objects (computers, cars, information).
- Withdrawal customers get their major gratification from interacting with ideas (thoughts, concepts, stories).
- Experimental customers rationalize their buying decisions by perceiving that what they bought is new, revolutionary, and innovative.
- Transitional customers rationalize their buying decisions by perceiving that what they bought is dependable and reliable.

- Traditional customers rationalize their buying decisions by perceiving that what they bought is cost-effective, a good deal, and worth the money.

In short:

- If your customer is tactile, you have to emphasize the *people* of your business.
- If your customer is neutral, you have to emphasize the *technology* of your business.
- If your customer is a withdrawal customer, you have to emphasize the *idea* of your business.
- If your customer is an experimental customer, you have to emphasize the *uniqueness* of your business.
- If your customer is transitional, you have to emphasize the *dependability* of your business.
- If your customer is traditional, you have to talk about the *financial competitiveness* of your business.

What your customers want is determined by who they are. Who they are is regularly demonstrated by what they do. Think about the customers with whom you do business. Ask yourself: In which of the categories would I place them? What do they do for a living?

If your customer is a mechanical engineer, for example, it's probably safe to assume he's a neutral customer. If another one of your customers is a cardiologist, she's probably tactile. Accountants tend to be traditional, and software engineers are often experimental.

Having an idea about which categories your customers may fall into is very helpful to figuring out what they want. Of course, there's no exact science to it, and human beings constantly defy stereotypes. So don't take my word for it. You'll want to make your own analysis of the customers you serve.

Confusion 2: How to Communicate Effectively with Your Customer

The next step in the customer satisfaction process is to decide how to magnify the characteristics of your business that are most likely to appeal to your preferred category of customer. That begins with what marketing people call your positioning strategy.

What do I mean by *positioning* your business? You position your business with words. A few well-chosen words to tell your customers exactly what they want to hear. In marketing lingo, those words are called your USP, or unique selling proposition.

For example, if you are targeting tactile customers (ones who love people), your USP could be: "Cozy Home Pest Control, where the comfort of people *really* counts!"

If you are targeting experimental customers (ones who love new, revolutionary things), your USP could be: "Smart Home Pest Control, where living on the edge is a way of life!" In other words, when they choose to schedule an installation with you, they can count on both your services and equipment to be on the cutting edge of the pest control industry.

Is this starting to make sense? Do you see how the ordinary things most contractors do to get customers can be done in a significantly more effective way?

Once you understand the essential principles of marketing the E-Myth way, the strategies by which you attract customers can make an enormous difference in your market share.

Confusion 3: How to Keep Your Customer Happy

Let's say you've overcome the first three confusions. Great. Now how do you keep your customer happy?

Very simple ... just keep your promise! And make sure your customer *knows* you kept your promise every step of the way.

In short, giving your customers what they think they want is the key to keeping your customers (or anyone else, for that matter) really happy.

If your customers need to interact with people (high touch, tactile), make certain that they do.

If they need to interact with things (high tech, neutral), make certain that they do.

If they need to interact with ideas (in their head, withdrawal), make certain that they do.

And so forth.

At E-Myth, we call this your *customer fulfillment system*. It's the step-by-step process by which you do the task you've contracted to do and deliver what you've promised—on time, every time.

But what happens when your customers are *not* happy? What happens when you've done everything I've mentioned here and your customer is still dissatisfied?

Confusion 4: How to Deal with Customer Dissatisfaction

If you have followed each step up to this point, customer dissatisfaction will be rare. But it can and will still occur—people are people, and some people will always find a way to be dissatisfied with something. Here's what to do about it:

- Always listen to what your customers are saying. And never interrupt while they're saying it.
- After you're sure you've heard all of your customer's complaint, make absolutely certain you understand what she said by phrasing a question such as: "Can I repeat what you've just told me, Ms. Harton, to make absolutely certain I understand you?"
- Secure your customer's acknowledgment that you have heard her complaint accurately.
- Apologize for whatever your customer thinks you did that dissatisfied her ... even if you didn't do it!

- After your customer has acknowledged your apology, ask her exactly what would make her happy.
- Repeat what your customer told you would make her happy, and get her acknowledgment that you have heard correctly.
- If at all possible, give your customer exactly what she has asked for.

You may be thinking, "But what if my customer wants something totally impossible?" Don't worry. If you've followed my recommendations to the letter, what your customer asks for will seldom seem unreasonable.

Confusion 5: Whom to Call a Customer

At this stage, it's important to ask yourself some questions about the kind of customers you hope to attract to your business:

- Which types of customers would you most like to do business with?
- Where do you see your real market opportunities?
- Who would you like to work with, provide services to, and position your business for?

In short, *it's all up to you.* No mystery. No magic. Just a systematic process for shaping your pest control company's future. But you must have the passion to pursue the process. And you must be absolutely clear about every aspect of it.

Until you know your customers as well as you know yourself.

Until all your complaints about customers are a thing of the past.

Until you accept the undeniable fact that customer acquisition and customer satisfaction are more science than art.

But unless you're willing to grow your business, you better not follow any of these recommendations. Because if you do what I'm suggesting, it's going to grow.

This brings us to the subject of growth. But first, let's see what Austin has to say about *customers*. ❧

16

The Simplest Way to Get the Best Customers

Austin Clark

"You'll never have a product or price advantage again. They can be too easily duplicated. But a strong customer service culture cannot be copied."

– Jerry Fritz

Michael's so right. As much as we love our clients, and even as well as we understand how to serve them, they can still offer up challenges when you aren't prepared.

After all, not all customers or clients are created equal. Our systems are designed to treat them equally, but sooner or later, you'll have the opportunity to serve someone who's outside the lines.

To some degree, we've already discussed that in an earlier chapter, but now I want to take it a step further – past the systems in your business and right to where the rubber meets the road – on the phone or face to face with a customer.

Why? Because a system that isn't used isn't a system in your business.

You've got to walk the walk, not just talk the talk.

When we asked you to identify your ideal client, it wasn't just an exercise in dreaming, it was a reality check; a line in the sand that clearly states, "At XYZ Pest Control, *this is what we do and who we do it for.*"

...And then you stand by that declaration.

Your ideal client isn't just your "dream client," he or she is also how you target your marketing.

Their beliefs are supported by your company's actions.

Their goals are too.

Your pest control company, to them at least, feels like it's aligned with their core values.

Identifying your ideal client is just one step. You not only need to know who they are, but also who they aren't, and how to attract the "right" ones and not get stuck with the wrong ones.

Anyone who's worked in the pest control industry has had some crazy experiences – some are gross, some are scary, but the worst ones are, in the end, the nightmare customers.

It's easy not to get caught up in the really weird ones. You or your team can usually identify the outliers in the first few minutes of a phone call. Your biggest customer challenges usually come from the ones that your systems can't catch right away.

If you take only one thing from this chapter, make it this one: catering to customers who are difficult to please creates more than just amusing stories and frustration; attracting and serving the wrong kind of customers can stunt the growth of your company.

Effectively, there are two types of problem customers. The first is just a bad person. Rude, loud, obnoxious, and likely unwilling to meet you even halfway. The second is harder to sniff out – they aren't "bad" in any real sense of the word, but they are extremely high maintenance. That makes them bad for business — specifically, they're bad for *your* business.

When I'm completely honest with myself, the vast majority of the customer problems we've ever had started because I had not clearly defined who our ideal client customers were and who they weren't. The good news, if you've been paying attention, is that even if you do have a system to weed out problem customers before they cause you a lot of grief, the system can and should be able to be changed and amended any time you identify how "problem" customers get into your system.

Remember my Error Log and Accountability Board?

If we see trends occurring in "problem" customers, we can address it quickly and take steps to prevent attracting those types of customers.

The hardest type of problem customer you'll ever deal with though, is the one you convince yourself to keep working with. Some years ago, I was having one of those days where things were just busy. We were shorthanded and under caffeinated, and I was getting worn out on the phone – taking calls, managing the office, and ... well, you get it.

This was the day that "Bob" called. Bob had a problem with rodents, something we handle all the time. No problem! This was going to be an easy new client - or so I thought.

As I've already told you, we have a system for onboarding new clients, and at that time, there were two main things we needed before turning Bob into a customer: an electronic payment method and a one or two-year initial service agreement.

Now, you might take checks, and that's fine, our reasoning is simple: not only is an electronic payment just an easier way of exchanging money, but it's also safer and less time-consuming than collecting cash or checks. Our team doesn't have to keep up with it, and payment is nearly instantaneous.

Requiring an initial service agreement enables us to handle things efficiently and quickly for the customer and the company, and just as importantly, it also allows us to systemize how we treat a property. First visit, we do this; the second visit, a few weeks later, our technicians do this; third visit, we've got this under control.

Not being able to follow our own processes would mean that every visit would need to be handled and billed individually. As a pest control owner, you know that if issues persist after the initial treatment, not having a service agreement can result in an angry customer who feels we're just trying to nickel and dime them for multiple trips and "emergencies."

Simple, right?

Nope. Not for Bob.

He had no desire to do either of those things, and, as someone who had tried to believe "the customer is always right," I caved.

After all, it was just "two little things," right?

We'd "WOW!" Bob with our service and he'd fall right in line.

You'd probably do it too. In fact, right now, you might be thinking, "What's the big deal? Bob isn't the worst kind of customer. Who cares if you have to make an exception to the rule? One more customer is one more customer, and that's the goal, right?"

Wrong.

The 80/20 Rule and the Problem with Bobs.

Most of us have heard of the 80/20 Rule, which basically states that 20% of your customers take up 80% of your time.

There are key reasons your systems and processes need to be in place: to prevent or minimize having these types of customers, and also, to identify how not to get trapped with them in the first place. Even if you don't have a "Bob" on your customer list, you're still spending time to address him and his kind by focusing on how to avoid them.

But you'd better do that, because Bob, and customers like him, refuse to go along with the procedures you have in place, and that forces you to reinvent the wheel every time you deal with them.

Back to my own "Bob." By refusing to provide electronic payment, we would have to spend time harassing Bob about his bill every time he used our services. That means someone would need to physically collect the payment from Bob AND we'd have to make a trip to the bank to deposit his check. Whoever processes payment information would also have to alter their procedure to account for an alternative form of payment.

As you can see, each variation from the system not only takes time, but because it's not systemized, it increases the likelihood that errors will occur.

In the case of Bob refusing to sign up for an initial service agreement, every treatment and interaction we have with him needed to be handled separately and existed outside of the system we created to make things run more smoothly.

You guessed it - all of that takes up more time, makes you less efficient, costs you more money, and adds to your employees' workload. What's worse is that it often ends up frustrating the customer because they never really get to see how well your systems actually work, and they often don't get the best level of service.

Obviously, you can't waste this much time worrying about the outliers, especially when they aren't adding anything to your actual profits. Remember that time you're spending chasing Bob's check? It's time you're taking away from your other customers.

That's really the core takeaway from this entire chapter: saying "yes" to one person can be the same thing as saying "no" to someone else. Be mindful of which customers you award with your time, energy, and other resources. When you agree to do business with "Bob," all the hard work you've put into coming up with a streamlined system to make things efficient and effective goes out the window.

To run a successful business, you need to be spending your time growing your company, improving your procedures, and expanding your employees' skills — not ignoring your systems for every client who asks.

Red Flags and Warning Signs

The problem with Bobs is they're just slightly out of alignment with your business systems, and you foolishly think you'll just be able to assimilate them with great service. In fact, as far as "difficult" customers go, Bob was pretty tame.

Here's the key takeaway - the customers that you need to guard yourself against are the ones who aren't as easily identifiable as problematic.

It's these types that populate your own 80/20 Rule. They seem nice and reasonable, so that makes them hard to identify, and they aren't necessarily rude about why they won't go along with your systems. In fact, they've got perfectly reasonable reasons, in many cases...

"My ID has been stolen, so I don't trust digital payments."

"I'll have to call you about scheduling, I can't think that far ahead."

"Pleeeeease, can you sneak me in this morning? We've got guests coming in from out of town, and I need to have the yard sprayed for the cookout this afternoon."

These are the customers who refuse to follow or go along with your key processes and procedures. It's not that they're necessarily trying to make things more difficult, but they do. When a client requires you to work outside of your normal system, it slows everyone down and it takes time away from you, your employees, and the rest of your customers.

This is one of the biggest reasons you need to have a system and a process – it tells you exactly what's next.

It also does something else: it supports you in your decision to say "no."

All you need to do is ask yourself (or teach your team to ask themselves), "Is what this customer or prospective customer asking me part of our process?"

If the answer is no, then they can confidently tell the client or prospect, "I'm sorry, at this time, we don't have the ability to service clients in that way. I'm sure there are other companies that can handle your job, but it doesn't appear we'll be able to help you."

No stress, no judgment, no challenges.

The fact is, you have to quit thinking about your pest control business as simply a series of optional steps and instead, imagine it's a conveyor belt in an automotive factory - each step of the process for assembling a product is efficiently timed and moves down the line in a particular order.

Can you imagine the chaos if someone decided that occasionally the product will need to be assembled in a slightly different manner, stopping the entire process in order to create a slightly different result?

This is how you need to view the systems and processes – and the results you expect from them - in your pest control business. Trying to create a slightly different product outside of your standard process is a huge waste of time and resources.

In short, you and your team – and your system – need to be able to identify customers who want you to reinvent the wheel early on and either convert them to your systems or kindly tell them, "Thanks but no thanks."

Remember, your ideal customer isn't someone who wants you to change the way you do things to accommodate them; they're the kind of person who appreciates the systems you've put in place to make both of your experiences better.

Just like most things, weeding out problematic customers gets easier over time. Once you start to recognize the same patterns with certain types of customers, you'll start to see the red flags much more quickly and clearly. Eventually, your familiarity with the warning signs will be sharp enough to help you avoid taking on those types of customers in the first place.

Identify Your Ideal Customer

After you understand how to avoid the customers that will harm your business, you can focus on the customers you want. If you're already running a company, you can start by looking at your current client base.

Who are your best customers?

What do they have in common?

Why are they such "good" customers?

If you analyze the customers who have been with you the longest and are the most profitable, you might begin to recognize some patterns.

For instance, our bread and butter comes from providing general residential pest control and any other pest-related service at a residential property. This might include termite, mosquito, or weed services. However, we also offer multifamily services for apartment buildings and industrial services. Despite that, our ideal customer remains the residential customer — this is what we're best at.

When we look at our best customers, they usually have some key things in common. They typically live in a single-family home, they have disposable income, and they recognize the time savings and value of having our team provide pest control and elimination services to them. We've also noticed many of our "ideal" clients tend to be the type that would also hire a pool cleaner, a window washing company, or a landscaping service.

In short, these customers already recognize the value of investing in the upkeep and maintenance of their homes, not necessarily doing it themselves.

Finding the things that your best customers have in common, and figuring out their reasons for wanting your services, can help you create a customer avatar that represents your ideal client.

Why? Because an avatar will help you understand the customer base where you'll want to focus your efforts: marketing, pricing, services, the works. Even more importantly, as your pest control business grows and expands geographically, knowing who you serve can allow you to capture new clients quickly in those new markets.

If you're at all serious about your pest control business, take a look at your current customers and ask yourself who you like to work with the most.

This isn't just about money. Ask yourself which customers really value and appreciate what you do and don't make you chase them for payments. Figure out the things that are really important to you and look at your customers who make those things possible.

After you've created one picture of an ideal client, keep identifying more of your favorite customers and putting together more customer avatars. This might represent new markets such as multifamily housing, or commercial properties, and so on. Or it might reflect a product designed for real estate investors with multiple properties.

What you're doing is getting to know your ideal client and going into detail with the profile you create.

Where do they shop? What restaurants do they go to? What sports are they into? What part of the country do they live in? Do they know a second language? Look for as many common characteristics of each group that you can find. The more details you can come up with, the better your avatars will be.

Getting this granular works both ways: Not only will it help you come up with avatars for your ideal clients, but it can also help you create profiles for the customers you want to avoid. You'll know where to spend your marketing budget. You'll have insight into a potential customer's pain points. You'll be confident in who you say "yes" to and who you're better off dismissing with a "no."

The end result of this work is to allow you to know who you serve and to build the systems that allow you to truly serve them and avoid the trap of problematic customer relationships. ❧

17

On the Subject of Growth

Michael E. Gerber

All organizations are hierarchical. At each level people serve under those above them. An organization is therefore a structured institution. If it is not structured, it is a mob. Mobs do not get things done, they destroy things.

—Theodore Levitt, Marketing for Business Growth

The rule of business growth says that every company, like every child, is destined to grow. Needs to grow. Is determined to grow.

Once you've created your pest control business, once you've shaped the idea of it, the most natural thing for it to do is to ... *grow!* And if you stop it from growing, it will die.

Once a pest control contractor has started a company, it's his or her job to help it grow. To nurture it and support it in every way. To infuse it with

- Purpose
- Passion
- Will
- Belief
- Personality
- Method

As your business grows, it naturally changes. And as it changes from a small business to something much bigger, you will begin to feel out of control. News flash: That's because you *are* out of control.

Your business *has* exceeded your know-how, sprinted right past you, and now it's taunting you to keep up. That leaves you two choices: Grow as big as your business demands you grow, or try to hold your business at its present level—at the level you feel most comfortable.

The sad fact is that most pest control owners do the latter. They try to keep their business small, securely within their comfort zone. Doing what they know how to do, what they feel most comfortable doing. It's called playing it safe.

But as the business grows, the number, scale, and complexity of tasks will grow, too, until they threaten to overwhelm the contractor. More people are needed. More space. More money. Everything seems to be happening at the same time. A hundred balls are in the air at once.

As I've said throughout this book: Most business owners are not entrepreneurs. They aren't true businesspeople at all, but technicians suffering from an entrepreneurial seizure. Their philosophy of coping with the workload can be summarized as "just do it," rather than figuring out how to get it done through other people using innovative systems to produce consistent results.

Given most contractors' inclination to be the master juggler in their business, it's not surprising that as complexity increases, as work expands beyond their ability to do it, as money becomes more elusive, they are just holding on, desperately juggling more and more balls. In the end, most collapse under the strain.

You can't expect your business to stand still. You can't expect your business to stay small. A company that stays small and depends on you to do everything isn't a company—it's a job!

Yes, just like your children, your business must be allowed to grow, to flourish, to change, to become more than it is. In this way, it will match your vision. And you know all about vision, right? You better. It's what you do best!

Do you feel the excitement? You should. After all, you know what your business *is* but not what it *can be*.

It's either going to grow or die. The choice is yours, but it is a choice that must be made. If you sit back and wait for change to overtake you, you will always have to answer no to this question: Are you ready?

That brings us to the subject of *change*. But first, let's see what Austin has to say about *growth*. ✤

CHAPTER

18

The Journey of Growth

Austin Clark

"Companies that grow for the sake of growth or that expand into areas outside their core business strategy often stumble. On the other hand, companies that build scale for the benefit of their customers and shareholders more often succeed over time."
—Jamie Dimon, President and CEO of JPMorgan Chase

Here's a hard fact: Growth is a part of your business. If you refuse to address and embrace growth, you don't own a business, you own a job – and it's a terrible one because your responsibilities never end. The owner who decides to run their business this way is simply, as Michael says, "a Technician suffering from an entrepreneurial seizure."

Since you've read this far, I think it's safe to say you're interested in growing your company for any number of reasons. Maybe it's to leave a legacy, maybe it's to finally be done with field work, maybe it's because your longer-term goals include selling your pest control business.

...But *truly* growing your business is hard work.

It sucks up tons of cash, loads of time, and – most importantly for us as business owners – it's often a steep learning curve as we move into areas or markets we don't intuitively know from our personal experiences.

We've got to learn how to collect and trust data, and we have to come to grips with the fact that growth means we're going to have to build a team and a company that runs on systems, not just "experience."

A few years ago, I received a call from a venture capitalist who wanted to discuss buying the company. This isn't unusual, and I don't usually call them back, but I had some questions of my own, and that phone call resulted in a very valuable conversation.

Now, I had no intention of selling, and I made that very clear to him at the outset of our call. But I also told him that I did want to understand a little bit more about how his firm evaluated companies, whether it was a home service company like ours, or a digital marketing agency, or any other type of growing business.

What I learned that day had a HUGE impact on how I looked at growth and how I would execute in the years to come.

As the voice on the other end of the line told me, investors and venture capitalists are looking first and foremost for growth *potential*. How they can add value to the company through their own actions and experiences. Don't be misled by that – they're not going to do the work; they're going to improve the systems *you've got in place*, or add their own, and maximize the value of the brand you've built.

Most importantly, this gentleman shared with me that any company looking for real growth – and for a potential sale in the future – should focus on their profits, their cashflow, their COGS, and their EBITDA. Remember those? Lastly, he told me they absolutely DON'T want to buy a business that relies on its owner. A business that relies on a single person is just a job with bad hours.

He left me with this thought, "Austin, all the things that would make your company, or any company, more desirable for a firm to purchase are the same things that would make your company more profitable today."

In other words, an attractive business should regularly raise rates and adjust pricing to keep up with costs and inflation. The more valuable your company is today, the more valuable it will be to an investment firm in the future.

Growth Is Just Adding Value

Everything we've discussed so far is designed to foster growth in your business, but it also adds value. Think of all of those difficult or time-consuming tasks that you've been putting off — firing bad customers, raising your prices, creating new systems to handle everything from hiring to scheduling to billing.

If you don't do them, the firm that purchases your company will, and they'll be the ones who profit from it. Companies don't purchase other companies to lose money.

In my own experience, many of the pest control owners I speak with share that part of their long-term goal is to sell the company. If that's you too, you not only have to be attractive to them, you need to begin taking action to do the things that will make your company more valuable and more profitable.

You're probably thinking, "How exactly do I grow my company without running my profits to the ground?"

Unfortunately, there is no single trick or gimmick that will make you successful. In order to boost your revenue now and in the future, you have to create foundational growth. We've talked about that in some of the previous chapters, and while it might sound like a cliche and even a bit old-fashioned, the best way to achieve foundational growth is to take care of your customers. That's because when you take care of your customers, they take care of you by continuing to do business with your company and referring other people to do the same.

Now take that to the logical next step, and the way you do that is to create the systems that take care of them.

…That supports great customer service.

…That supports clients to easily find and work with you.

…That supports healthy profits and cash flow.

…That supports your ability to find and hire good people to create a great outcome.

So, the logical first step of growth is to ensure that your clientele feels taken care of before you go spend the money to generate new leads. This will give you the disposable income you need for marketing, lead conversion, and training and save you from working harder to replace the revenue that is going out the back door.

Doubling *Something*

If you want to achieve real growth and increase your revenue at the same time, you have two options: you can either double your customer base, or you can keep your same customer base and double their rates. It's easy to lose money when all your sales are captured from only new customers, since the cost of generating those new customers can be extreme. Because of this, I would recommend option number two: raising your rates.

Of course, as any good business owner knows, you can't raise rates just for the heck of raising rates. If you want to increase your pricing, you'll have to offer something of value in return. Finding the right balance between your prices and your services is paramount.

Consumers aren't stupid; they work hard for their money and they're very intelligent about where they spend it. So for them to entrust you — or Netflix, or any other company — with their hard-earned dollars, they must be getting value in return.

There are a few ways to go about raising your prices in order to provide the best value and service to your customers, but the test I like to use is to ask these two questions:

1.   If you were to double your rates right now, would all of your customers cancel your service?

2. If so, what would it look like to provide so much value to your customers that if you did double your rates, not one of them would cancel?

Depending on the types of services you offer in your pest control company, this could mean anything from offering a new product or service to providing a more premium quality of service with your current offerings.

The results though, can allow you to effectively double your rates and still provide incredible value to your clients. Bear in mind, it's not just the costs to your customer we're talking about here either.

It's also about the profitability of any given product or service.

Think in terms of packaging services, annualizing contracts, automating bill pay and scheduling, and so on. By getting down into the real "nitty gritty" of those costs and values, you may find, for example, that with automated bill pay and an annual contract, you and your team save seven hours per customer each year.

Thus, the profitability of a revised service package may, in reality, have the same effect as doubling your rates.

Creating a Growth Plan

Remember what I said before about growth sucking cash? This is especially true when you start to offer new and expanding services. I've already shared some of the missteps we've made in the past, and as I've talked to the owners of pest control companies all over the country, they've fallen victim to the same errors.

It's incredibly tempting to be everything for everyone, and when customers start asking for a new or additional service or product, you may think that the best option for your business is to say, "yes."

What you want to do is master doing one thing first. When you've gotten that dialed in, you'll move on to the next thing. I choose to think of it as "Fail fast and fail forward." By that, I mean that even if an idea doesn't work out, it still has a value. Maybe your test of a new product didn't work out well, but it gave you valuable data and metrics on a specific area of your business that can be used. In any event, you MUST be highly intentional about the things you decide to add. Make sure your reasons for adding a service align with the wants and needs of your ideal customers.

Take us, for example. It took us years to finally begin offering termite treatments and we did that for one reason: so many of our customers really wanted that service.

We didn't rush into it the first time a customer mentioned it, or the second time, or the tenth time. Not even the hundredth time. Our customers were requesting termite services for years before we determined that adding that service would be a worthwhile investment.

From that data, we could create a termite treatment package that aligned with our core values regarding quality and pricing, and it was a successful – and relatively easy – step in our growth.

When we launched the termite program, we had reliable data from clients, we had an accurate projection of the profitability, and we had a specific goal – in this case, half a million dollars annually.

The income and profits from our core business allowed us to fund the new program, and it also guaranteed we would continue to generate profits regardless of the success of our expansion into termite treatment.

Since we had set those benchmarks and created a plan, termite treatments proved to be a very worthwhile investment helping us to grow, expand, and boost the value of our business.

All growth is not based on traditional growth strategies though. Once I had established our relationship with our customers and mastered the art of pricing and expanding our services, I was able to move onto some "sexier" strategies.

Direct sales (which had a few false starts) have proven to be incredibly valuable to our growth trajectory. The same with digital marketing and social media.

...Ironically, we've also begun to focus on acquisitions, which has allowed us to partner with companies in cities all over the United States.

No matter the strategy though, make sure it has a valuable return on investment. The best way to do this is to track *everything*.

For example, if you create a Facebook campaign - whether you're investing $1 or $10,000 - you should track how many views you get, what your click-through rate looks like, and how much of your traffic converted into sales. This way, you have an accurate idea of how valuable this investment really was for the growth of your company.

Remember though, click-through rates and sales numbers aren't the only types of ROI that contribute to your company's value. While a financial return is critical, raising awareness is also important for growth. Strategies like radio ads and billboards may be slower to provide a return, but when someone is driving down the road or listening to a radio station, these campaigns will stick in their minds — and you never know how many phone calls or purchases will follow.

So don't be afraid to experiment with a variety of different strategies and don't hesitate to take some risks – that's why your growth plan is based on the solid foundation of the business systems you've created and the data you've researched – but also?

Hire an expert.

I did this when we first began using various types of digital marketing in the early days of the company, and even though the price tag was over $50,000, I had confidence in the team I had hired.

They did a great job – not only setting our expectations, but also by being able to show us why this strategy would produce before another one.

As nerve-wracking as it was, I'm glad I stuck with it. Year over year, our leads tripled and our sales doubled. All because of that one campaign.

Growing to Avoid Extinction

Several years ago, I read *The Zappos Experience* by Joseph Michelli and it was incredibly insightful. There are not many companies that have seen the success Zappos has in the past several years. Within a decade, the company grew from zero revenue to a billion-dollar valuation *and* an acquisition from Amazon.

While the whole book was filled with value, one of the most critical things I took away from it was the importance of one of Zappos' core values: embrace and drive change.

For me, thinking about "change" immediately brings to mind how much we – as humans – have changed as a species. Over those thousands of years, we've changed in almost every way: from where we live to how we communicate, to what we value as individuals.

The reason for that change? If we hadn't changed, humans would have gone extinct.

"Change" is synonymous with "growth," especially when you're running a business.

More importantly though, think about growth in your pest control business.

Most of the time, it's been painful, and for one big reason: It's always depended on you!

If you take nothing else from this book, take this: Creating and implementing systems in your pest control company is the only real way you can grow.

…And I hear it all the time, "Austin, there's just not enough time in the day for me to work on my business! You don't understand!"

Actually, I do, and if you've committed to truly growing your pest control business, you need to stop believing two lies right now:

1.   That people are your most important asset.
2.   That time is your most important advantage.

The truth is your *processes* are your most important asset. THAT'S what truly distinguishes great companies. You need to do away with the old ways of thinking about "people" as individuals. That's not to say they aren't critical to your company – people are.

...But how those people deliver and produce results is far more important.

Identify that, and then learn to repeat it again and again and your pest control company's growth will be virtually assured. If your business model depended on Fred, when Fred stops producing, Fred's gone and so is the success he brings.

In a company driven by systems, *Fred is never the problem, the system is.* When you begin to pay attention to the way *your company* does the work instead of *who* does the work, you can really begin to grow.

Now how can you start embracing and driving growth with your business?

For starters, you need to allow your pest control business to move into the modern world. To this day, I'm shocked at how many owners of pest control companies are still operating their companies like it's 1985.

Paying with checks, invoicing by mail, marketing in the phone book, and not capitalizing on social media.

Try to imagine any other industry today that doesn't embrace social media. While small local companies with strong customer ties might be able to hold on for dear life using tactics that have been eclipsed in the last two decades, the truth is, they can never have the same success or longevity as their technology-savvy competition.

In other words, technology is advancing exponentially. And if pest control operators can't – or won't - keep up, then they'll be left behind.

Like Zappos, you should be embracing change and open to growth. Change is inevitable, whether it's with business, or technology, or even you. Change gives us the opportunity for growth, so you have to be prepared to react when it happens. Are you going to resist it? Or, are you going to roll with it and become a trendsetter?

Again, this is where the true value of a systems-based company begins to shine.

The Amazon Effect

There are loads of factors impacting your company's ability to grow and even conduct business these days. Think about the shift we've seen in the service industries based on the consumer's experience elsewhere. To put it simply: Consumers know what they want, and they want it *now*.

This change once again loops back to technology. More specifically, I believe it can be traced to platforms like Amazon, which are providing goods and services quicker and easier than ever before.

On Amazon, you can order something with the click of a button and have it delivered to your door within a day. This has changed how consumers expect to be taken care of - they expect the same efficient service wherever they shop, including in service-based industries like pest control.

They also expect things to be done right the first time. There are more options than ever for every type of business, so value is top-of-mind for today's consumers.

As long as you can identify the changes and meet the evolving needs of your consumers, you can build a business that not only lasts, it also can grow year after year. We've had to roll with a lot of changes throughout the years — and they have only improved our service.

We also have a huge responsibility to deliver a service that provides value for every dollar a client spends. In most cases, that means adapting to changes in the industry and updating our business to reflect the evolving needs of our customers.

Our rates can easily be considered a "premium" versus most of the competitors in our markets, and we've been able to maintain these prices because we always deliver the value to match.

How do we do this exactly?

You already know the answer – we take our profits and reinvest them into our business. This way, we have up-to-date technology, better-trained people, premium products, and a world-class customer experience that relies on a proven *system*.

We've worked hard to implement technology into our systems, too. For example, one of our favorites is a fully integrated CRM called PestRoutes that acts as a CRM software. "CRM" stands for "Customer Relationship Management" and it stores all of our customers' information in one place. With it, and another piece called Podium, we can handle nearly any type of communication with our clients - whether that's email, texts, or calls. It's important to realize, though, that a software, in and of itself, isn't going to solve all of your challenges, but you, as an operator, need to be open to embracing the solutions the right CRM can offer your pest control business.

Let's face it, the next generation of customers are millennials and generation Z, and we know they'd much rather communicate with a simple message versus a long drawn-out conversation.

However, our use of this technology doesn't mean that we're afraid to fall back on those more traditional forms of communication as well. For our customers who prefer a phone call, we still pick up the phone. For our clients who prefer email, we still check our inbox.

Ultimately, our purpose is to improve the lives of our customers, and we can only do that if we grow. By respecting how our clients want to communicate, for example, we don't isolate one customer base, no matter if they're from an older generation or a more tech-savvy one. We have customers who are 85 years old, and we have customers who are 18 years old. They come from all walks of life and live in all types of homes, from multimillion-dollar houses to small boats. At the end of the day, we want to serve as many customers as we can with the specific services that we provide.

How to Avoid Going Extinct

Similar to the ancestors who came before us, our consequence for avoiding growth is extinction. While you may not go extinct from refusing to embrace the latest technology and trends, your business sure will.

Take Blockbuster for example. Today, only one Blockbuster remains from what was once a huge, nationwide franchise.

Why? The easy answer is that they lost all of their customers to Netflix. And while that's true, it really comes down to the value that Netflix provided that Blockbuster couldn't.

If you remember, Blockbuster had quite a few pain points. Most notably were the late fees, which seemed to accumulate exponentially week over week. People also didn't want to go anywhere to get a movie for their Friday or Saturday night in. They especially didn't want to go and walk around a store if they didn't know whether the movie they wanted was available.

When a new movie came out, they didn't want to line up outside the door in order to get a copy - or wait three weeks until the demand had decreased.

And despite these customer complaints and the new technology that was becoming available, Blockbuster didn't evolve to meet the market. Meanwhile, Netflix was paying attention to the changes that were happening and strategically transformed from a rent-by-mail DVD service to a movie and television streaming service.

As you now know, Blockbuster went extinct, and the rest is history.

The same goes for taxis. For ages, consumers had been complaining about taxi services. They felt vulnerable about who was giving them a ride, or they felt ripped off by how much a ride ended up costing.

Enter Uber and Lyft. Using innovative technology, these companies addressed all of these complaints and more. Now I can't even remember the last time I took a taxi!

What makes these companies still relevant today is the fact that they haven't stopped changing and evolving to meet the demands of the time.

During the global pandemic in 2020, a ride-sharing service could have easily gone extinct if it hadn't quickly adapted to the changing market. However, Uber and Lyft were quick to update their services and maintain value for their customers. All it took was a small checkbox reminding customers that they had to wear a mask and comply with safety regulations in order to use the service, and an open mind to offer value-added ideas like delivery services.

Imagine trying to do this with taxis!

Growth Is About a Successful Exit

Remember: When you embrace and drive change, you can build a stronger business that can continue to grow year after year and will last the test of time. Most importantly, you can provide real value for your customers.

This is the secret to success for Zappos, Netflix, Uber, Lyft, and, of course, us.

Not only does this help you stay in business longer, but growth and longevity also position you as an industry leader.

You're the first one to adopt new technologies.

You're providing the services that your customers rave about.

You're the trendsetter in your field.

As you continue to grow and build your business, try to keep an eye out for where you can change and evolve to meet the demands of your market. Instead of running away from change, look for ways you can achieve it faster. Just as importantly, recognize that growth and change are also setting your and your company up for the next owner.

Here's a hard truth: you won't own your company forever. Maybe the next generation of your family will operate it, maybe you'll sell it, maybe you'll partner with another company.

Despite all the work I've put toward growing my company and boosting its value, I still haven't sold it. Instead, I've taken on the role of that person on the phone who I spoke to all those years ago. Now I acquire pest control businesses so I can keep improving and growing the brand.

What I've learned along the way is that you should always stay focused on the value of your business. You never know when you're going to want to sell it; but, when you do, you want to get the best price.

One business that we acquired was owned by a man named Randy. He had been in business for thirty years and had never thought that he could sell the company for the price I was willing to offer. But, because he had maintained a profitable, valuable, and growth-oriented business for all those years, he was able to make a successful exit.

And now, Randy is living the good life.

The right growth strategy can set you up for that too! ❧

CHAPTER

19

On the Subject of Change

Michael E. Gerber

Our Leaders of today need the philosophy of the past, paired with the scientific knowledge and technology of tomorrow.

—Anders Indset

So your pest control company is growing. That means, of course, that it's also changing. Which means it's driving you and everyone in your life crazy.

That's because, to most people, change is a diabolical thing. Tell most people they've got to change, and their first instinct is to crawl directly into a hole. Nothing threatens their existence more than change. Nothing cements their resistance more than change. Nothing!

Yet for the past thirty-five years, that's exactly what I've been proposing to small business owners: the need to change. Not for the sake of change itself, but for the sake of their lives.

I've talked to countless business owners whose hopes weren't being realized through their business; whose lives were consumed

149

by work; who slaved increasingly longer hours for decreasing pay; whose dissatisfaction grew as their enjoyment shriveled; whose business had become the worst job in the world; whose money was out of control; whose employees were a source of never-ending hassles, just like their customers, their bank, and, increasingly, even their family.

More and more, these contractors spent their time alone, dreading the unknown and anxious about the future. And even when they were with people, they didn't know how to relax. Their mind was always on the job. They were distracted by work, by the thought of work. By the fear of falling behind.

And yet, when confronted with their condition and offered an alternative, most of the same owners strenuously resisted it. They assumed that if there were a better way of doing business, they already would have figured it out. They derived comfort from knowing what they believed they already knew. They accepted the limitations of being a pest control owner; or the truth about people; or the limitations of what they could expect from their customers, their employees, their subcontractors, their bankers—even their family and friends.

In short, most contractors I've met over the years would rather live with the frustrations they already have than risk enduring new frustrations.

Isn't that true of most people you know? Rather than opening up to the infinite number of possibilities life offers, they prefer to shut their lives down to respectable limits. After all, isn't that the most reasonable way to live?

I think not. I think we must learn to let go. I think that if you fail to embrace change, it will inevitably destroy you.

Conversely, by opening yourself to change, you give your pest control business the opportunity to get the most from your talents.

Let me share with you an original way to think about change, about life, about who we are and what we do. About the stunning notion of expansion and contraction.

Contraction versus Expansion

"Our salvation," a wise man once said, "is to allow." That is, to be open, to let go of our beliefs, to change. Only then can we move from a point of view to a viewing point.

That wise man was Thaddeus Golas, the author of a small, powerful book entitled *The Lazy Man's Guide to Enlightenment* (Seed Center, 1971).

Among the many inspirational things he had to say was this compelling idea:

The basic function of each being is expanding and contracting. Expanded beings are permeative; contracted beings are dense and impermeative. Therefore each of us, alone or in combination, may appear as space, energy, or mass, depending on the ratio of expansion to contraction chosen, and what kind of vibrations each of us expresses by alternating expansion and contraction. Each being controls his or her own vibrations.

In other words, Golas tells us that the entire mystery of life can be summed up in two words: *expansion* and *contraction*. He goes on to say:

We experience expansion as awareness, comprehension, understanding, or whatever we wish to call it.

When we are completely expanded, we have a feeling of total awareness, of being one with all life.

At that level we have no resistance to any vibrations or interactions of other beings. It is timeless bliss, with unlimited choice of consciousness, perception, and feeling.

When a (human) being is totally contracted, he is a mass particle, completely imploded.

To the degree that he is contracted, a being is unable to be in the same space with others, so the contraction is felt as fear, pain, unconsciousness, ignorance, hatred, evil, and a whole host of strange feelings.

At an extreme (of contraction, a human being) has the feeling of being completely insane, of resisting everyone and everything, of being unable to choose the content of his consciousness.

Of course, these are just the feelings appropriate to mass vibration levels, and he can get out of them at any time by expanding, by letting go of all resistance to what he thinks, sees, or feels.

Stay with me here. Because what Golas says is profoundly important. When you're feeling oppressed, overwhelmed, exhausted by more than you can control—contracted, as Golas puts it—you can change your state to one of expansion.

According to Golas, the more contracted we are, the more threatened we are by change; the more expanded we are, the more open we are to change.

In our most enlightened—that is, open—state, change is as welcome as non-change. Everything is perceived as a part of ourselves. There is no inside or outside. Everything is one thing. Our sense of isolation is transformed to a feeling of ease, of light, of joyful relationship with everything.

As infants, we didn't even think of change in the same way, because we lived those first days in an unthreatened state. Insensitive to the threat of loss, most young children are only aware of *what is*. Change is simply another form of *what is*. Change just *is*.

However, when we are in our most contracted—that is, closed—state, change is the most extreme threat. If the known is what I have, then the unknown must be what threatens to take away what I have. Change, then, is the unknown. And the unknown is fear. It's like being between trapezes.

- To the fearful, change is threatening because things may get worse.
- To the hopeful, change is encouraging because things may get better.
- To the confident, change is inspiring because the challenge exists to improve things.

If you are fearful, you see difficulties in every opportunity. If you are fear-free, you see opportunities in every difficulty.

Fear protects what I have from being taken away. But it also disconnects me from the rest of the world. In other words, fear keeps me separate and alone.

Here's the exciting part of Golas's message: With this new understanding of contraction and expansion, we can become completely attuned to where we are at all times.

If I am afraid, suspicious, skeptical, and resistant, I am in a contracted state. If I am joyful, open, interested, and willing, I am in an expanded state. Just knowing this puts me on an expanded path. Always remembering this, Golas says, brings enlightenment, which opens me even more.

Such openness gives me the ability to freely access my options. And taking advantage of options is the best part of change. Just as there are infinite ways to greet a customer, there are infinite ways to run your business. If you believe Thaddeus Golas, your most exciting option is to be open to all of them.

Because your life is lived on a continuum between the most contracted and most expanded—the most closed and most open—states, change is best understood as the movement from one to the other, and back again.

Most small business owners I've met see change as a thing-in-itself, as something that just happens to them. Most experience change as a threat. Whenever change shows up at the door, they quickly slam it. Many bolt the door and pile up the furniture. Some even run for their gun.

Few of them understand that change isn't a thing-in-itself, but rather the manifestation of many things. You might call it the revelation of all possibilities. Think of it as the ability at any moment to sacrifice what we are for what we could become.

Change can either challenge us or threaten us. It's our choice. Our attitude toward change can either pave the way to success or throw up a roadblock.

Change is where opportunity lives. Without change we would stay exactly as we are. The universe would be frozen still. Time would end.

At any given moment, we are somewhere on the path between a contracted and expanded state. Most of us are in the middle of the journey, neither totally closed nor totally open. According to Golas, change is our movement from one place in the middle toward one of the two ends.

Do you want to move toward contraction or toward enlightenment? Because without change, you are hopelessly stuck with what you've got.

Without change,

- we have no hope;
- we cannot know true joy;
- we will not get better; and
- we will continue to focus exclusively on what we have and the threat of losing it.

All of this negativity contracts us even more, until, at the extreme closed end of the spectrum, we become a black hole so dense that no light can escape.

Sadly, the harder we try to hold on to what we've got, the less able we are to do so. So we try still harder, which eventually drags us even deeper into the black hole of contraction.

Are you like that? Do you know anybody who is?

Think of change as the movement between where we are and where we're not. That leaves only two directions for change: either moving forward or slipping backward. We either become more contracted or more expanded.

The next step is to link change to how we feel. If we feel afraid, change is dragging us backward. If we feel open, change is pushing us forward.

Change is not a thing in itself, but a movement of our consciousness. By tuning in, by paying attention, we get clues to the state of our being.

Change, then, is not an outcome or something to be acquired. Change is a shift of our consciousness, of our being, of our humanity, of our attention, of our relationship with all other beings in the universe.

We are either "more in relationship" or "less in relationship." Change is the movement in either of those directions. The exciting part is that *we possess the ability to decide which way we go ... and to know in the moment which way we're moving.*

Closed, open. ... Open, closed. Two directions in the universe. The choice is yours.

Do you see the profound opportunity available to you? What an extraordinary way to live!

Enlightenment is not reserved for the sainted. Rather, it comes to us as we become more sensitive to ourselves. Eventually, we become our own guides, alerting ourselves to our state, moment by moment: *open ... closed ... open ... closed.*

Listen to your inner voice, your ally, and feel what it's like to be open and closed. Experience the instant of choice in both directions.

You will feel the awareness growing. It may be only a flash at first, so be alert. This feeling is accessible, but only if you avoid the black hole of contraction.

Are you afraid that you're totally contracted? Don't be—it's doubtful. The fact that you're still reading this book suggests that you're moving in the opposite direction.

You're more like a running back seeking the open field. You can see the opportunity gleaming in the distance. In the open direction.

Understand that I'm not saying that change itself is a point on the path; rather, it's the all-important movement.

Change is *in you*, not *out there.*

What path are you on? The path of liberation? Or the path of crystallization?

As we know, change can be for the better or for the worse.

If change is happening *inside* of you, it is for the worse only if you remain closed to it. The key, then, is your attitude—your acceptance or rejection of change. Change can be for the better only if you accept it. And it will certainly be for the worse if you don't.

Remember, change is nothing in itself. Without you, change doesn't exist. Change is happening inside of each of us, giving us clues to where we are at any point in time.

Rejoice in change, for it's a sign you are alive.

Are we open? Are we closed? If we're open, good things are bound to happen. If we're closed, things will only get worse.

According to Golas, it's as simple as that. Whatever happens defines where we are. *How* we are is *where* we are. It cannot be any other way.

For change is life.

Charles Darwin wrote, "It is not the strongest of the species that survive, nor the most intelligent, but the one that proves itself most responsive to change."

The growth of your pest control business, then, is its change. Your role is to go with it, to be with it, to share the joy, embrace the opportunities, meet the challenges, learn the lessons.

Remember, there are three kinds of people: (1) those who make things happen, (2) those who let things happen, and (3) those who wonder what the hell happened. The people who make things happen are masters of change. The other two are its victims.

Which type are you?

The Big Change

If all this is going to mean anything to the life of your company, you have to know when you're going to leave it. At what point, in your company's rise from where it is now to where it can ultimately grow, are you going to sell it? Because if you don't have a clear picture of when you want out, your business is the master of your destiny, not the reverse.

As we stated earlier, the most valuable form of money is equity, and unless your business vision includes your equity and how you will use it to your advantage, you will forever be consumed by your business.

Your business is potentially the best friend you ever had. It is your business's nature to serve you, so let it. If, however, you are not a wise steward, if you do not tell your business what you expect from it, it will run rampant, abuse you, use you, and confuse you.

Change. Growth.Equity.

Focus on the point in the future when you will take leave of your business. Now reconsider your goals in that context. Be specific. Write them down.

Skipping this step is like tiptoeing through earthquake country. Who can say where the fault line is waiting? And who knows exactly when your whole world may come crashing down around you?

Which brings us to the subject of *time*. But first, let's see what Austin has to say regarding *change*. ♣

CHAPTER

20

The Real Work of Change

Austin Clark

"The world is changing very fast. Big will not beat small anymore. It will be the fast beating the slow."

—Rupert Murdoch

L et's be honest – Michael's observations about expansion and contraction are spot on. You and I have both seen it and lived it.

Maybe you're living a little too much of it right now.

I speak with a lot of business owners and entrepreneurs all over the country, and in those conversations, I can tell a lot about the individual based on how they talk about their business.

Take the following two sentences:

"We've been able to show solid growth in this market for twelve straight quarters."

"I've been so busy I don't even know which way is up."

On the surface, both sound like business is going well.

But, if you think about the idea of expansion and contraction, which of those two sentences above comes from an entrepreneur who is expanding and one who is contracting?

To truly embrace the E-Myth mentality is to embrace change and expansion, but that seems especially hard for the owners of many pest control companies. In my experience though, the real secret to embracing change in your company – and, let's be honest, in your life - comes down to three core focuses:

Your vision, the change, and the strategy you'll use to bring about that change in your business. Let's take a harder look at each of those, and how they impact change in your pest control business.

Understanding Your Vision

Traditionally, Michael has defined the Vision of the Entrepreneur as "the form your company must take in order to produce a desired Great Result." It's one part business plan, and one part operating system. The operating system gives you the basis to build and develop the plan.

It's really no big deal to find that operating system. At its core, you're identifying an existing one that works and modifying it to suit your business.

You could use the one I've shared here – the one that's made us successful, or you could take a page right from Michael's playbook and use McDonalds'. Don't believe me?

Think about all the things that McDonalds does right every day – millions and millions of meals served around the world, all run by systems that are managed by ordinary people. A chef doesn't lovingly handcraft that Quarter Pounder, a regular person uses a system to cook it.

Your pest control business could be incredibly successful mimicking the same essential systems McDonalds uses right now.

The system you choose isn't important; what *is* important is having one. Amateurs have a goal, professionals have a process.

However, the best system in the world will never work until you have a vision to drive it. What exactly do I mean by vision? Ask yourself where you want your company to be.

Don't just imagine "success" as some abstract idea, *define it.*

Visualize it with all your senses. What does it look like, feel like, smell like, taste like, and sound like?

What's an average day like when you've built your pest control company properly and embraced not only growth, but also change?

When you've accepted *expansion*?

These are the same kinds of visualization strategies that athletes use when they're working on peak performance goals. They imagine what they want in great detail. For instance, when their goal is to win, they consider what it feels like to hold the trophy and what it sounds like when they hit the winning shot. They close their eyes and picture the expressions on people's faces in the crowd. They imagine the cool sweat on the back of their neck and the taste of salt, and they feel their heartbeat jump.

In business, it's no different. The more you know about where you want to be, the easier it will be to get there.

And it might be easy to say, "Well, Austin, I just own a pest control company in Sioux City. Dad started it and I'm stuck with it. There's no game winner here…"

That's the wrong way to look at it – that assumes that the entirety of your life is the business you do – and that's exactly what this book is designed to move you past.

Your pest control business is bigger than you, and you are bigger than it. To the extent you'll create a vision of your business that doesn't rely on *you*, that's the extent of the success you'll have.

Steve Jobs didn't build Macs or iPhones. He built Apple.

Ray Kroc didn't flip burgers or cook French fries. He built McDonalds.

You don't exist to kill bugs. You exist to build your business.

That's the Vision … and that's where the change must come in.

Telling the Story

If you truly have a vision, the first rule is you have to share it. Think of your team, think of your customers, think of your banker, or your creditors, or your investors.

Let others know what it is and bring the vividness of your vision to everyone in your company. It's something that you should constantly be speaking about and reinforcing. It's more than simply a pest control company – it's your story.

We can liken this vision – this goal – to the view from a mountain, and in that respect, if the place you want to get to is the top of a mountain, you want to show everyone that mountain top.

Describe what it looks like up there at the top.

Talk about how it feels and how the water tastes.

Explain the sound of the wind and the smell of the trees.

Share all of those sensory elements that you've imagined for yourself so it can become just as real for everyone else. And do so constantly.

You'll quickly see – as I have – who is expanding and who is contracting.

Not everyone on your team will share that vision, and that's okay. Why? Because they're people!

The vision you have for your company no longer relies on people; it relies on systems and processes. Certainly, as we've discussed, it needs people to do the work, but the overall operating system you're creating allows you to use "good" people – not highly skilled or even experienced people – and it allows you to be outrageously successful.

From this vision must come action though, and that action can be summed up in one word: change.

People *hate* change.

Your team, your partners, your investors and creditors, your customers – invariably, people hate change.

…But it's inevitable.

Over and over again, in these pages, I've shared how often we encounter pest control companies that haven't changed in decades, even though nearly everything else has.

By now, I've listed dozens of ways we've sought and implemented "change" to the old business model followed by so many pest control companies, but I really want to talk about change in a different place.

The mind of the entrepreneur.

Imagine someone who's scaled their pest control company to a certain point, and then it stops growing. Maybe it's $100,000 or a half million. Maybe it's a million or a few million. The amount doesn't matter. What *does* matter is that the company has hit a phase where it's not really growing anymore.

I see it all the time in family companies – Dad or Grandad never really shared their own vision – or even had one. They built themselves a job for any variety of reasons, and now a new generation has the business.

But no one ever told them it could be more than it's been for two, or three, or four decades.

No one ever told them it could be a regional or even a national company.

In all likelihood, it's because the business never had any real systems or processes, aside from the most basic ones, to collect the invoices and pay the bills. Usually, more robust systems are missing for a couple of reasons.

- No one ever thought they were needed.
- The owner wouldn't let anyone do it for them.

If you're actually willing to truly embrace change and create both a story worth telling and one worth living, you HAVE to stop believing the old adage that says, "If you want something done right, do it yourself." It's simply impossible to grow your business if you insist on trying to be the one who takes every phone call, responds to every email, and handles all the invoicing.

Budget yourself. Exchange your cash or other resources for time — but spend it wisely. Don't try and do everything on your own. And focus your time and energy where it belongs — on vision, growth, and strategy.

As an entrepreneur, your real work isn't writing every check. It's not making every phone call. It's not returning every text. It's not sitting in on every employee coaching session. It's not performing every job or making sure that all the shipments get out on time.

All of those things are important, and they need to be done, but they're not necessarily the most important things for *you* to be doing.

The True Work of The Entrepreneur

A story worth telling is a story that needs a hero.

That's you.

...But no one wants to hear how you bravely sprayed four houses today and drove home during rush hour.

Michael identified three different roles most business owners play in their companies – the Technician, the Manager, and the Entrepreneur.

While it's true that, in the beginning, you might have no choice but to be active in all three roles, one of the first steps for change is recognizing the value of every task you do.

Put a price on everything you do in your company, every day.

Technical work – actually treating homes or businesses, answering phones, creating invoices – might be worth $15-20/hour.

Managerial work – hiring, onboarding, employee reviews and so on – that's worth $20-$30/hour.

The true work of the Entrepreneur? Embracing and creating the systems for change and growth? That's CEO-level stuff. Professional fees, like $250-$1,000/hour.

The real entrepreneur is going to find himself, or herself, doing their absolute best to stay in the entrepreneurial area as much as possible.

How? Through change.

Changing the way they think about how work gets done.

Creating systems to allow them NOT to have to do the technical and managerial tasks ... with a notable "but."

"*But,*" that entrepreneur is not going to abdicate their responsibilities to just anyone. They'll create systems and processes to allow the technicians and managers of their business to know exactly what to do, and how to do it.

You cannot simply hire someone and disappear. You have to have taken the time and created the systems that effectively run the company. And when you do, you'll have the time to focus on the true work of the entrepreneur – identifying where and when change is coming and how your business will react to – and embrace – that change.

Some great examples are: identifying different lean initiatives inside the company, comparing different marketing opportunities, pursuing other pest control companies for purchase and expansion, identifying what changes need to be made in the various systems and processes in your company, and so on.

In short, these types of tasks are often things that will affect multiple people in your company. For instance, if you did something that saves every employee a few minutes, you can multiply the time you saved by the number of employees you have. Then multiply that number by however many days, weeks, or months that it will continue to save time.

It all adds up to a company that can change quickly – and expand.

Investing in People

If I'm honest with myself, the biggest changes we focus on within my company are in training. We're a bit fanatical about it, but in a healthy way. If you want to execute any plan or make any change, you need to train your staff.

When they know how to do their jobs, you can focus on yours, and when that happens, your business can thrive.

Our outlook is simple - training is an investment and not a cost. It offers us a tremendous competitive advantage - especially when most of the competition refuses to do it because they incorrectly calculate it as a cost, and they (somewhat foolishly) focus only on hiring the most highly skilled people, with little regard for how well those people can interact with others.

Carving out thirty minutes each day for training every single employee might seem like a lot, and most businesses are unwilling to even consider doing such a thing. Nonetheless, we've been doing that for the last decade and a half, and it's made a significant difference.

As I've shared before, this training extends into accountability, and working together as a team to identify errors and to figure out solutions to keep those issues from recurring has helped turn average people with a great attitude into a highly skilled workforce that really does work together.

When your employees are reviewing and fixing issues every week, you, as an owner and entrepreneur, end up putting out far fewer fires.

By making self-improvement a priority in your company and giving your employees the tools they need to continue to expand in their own skills and lives, you make that expansion and growth a part of the company culture.

When your staff improves — your company improves.

Entrepreneurs, Get to Work

Undoubtedly, you've heard the old saying, "If you give a man a fish, you feed him for a day. If you teach a man to fish, you feed him for a lifetime." While no one seems to know exactly where that originated, I think that saying sums up what an entrepreneur's real work is.

We have a responsibility to be successful, as we have a responsibility to continuously grow our businesses. Growth can only come from change, since change is really the only "sure thing" in business.

Many of us also want to teach people how to be successful, to inspire.

We want to give people the tools they need to thrive — in any role, in any environment, and in any place.

When you can encapsulate the entrepreneur's real work, and really set about doing it, you will be an inspiration, and there's nothing that your employees won't do for you. If you can teach your staff and show them how to make money and how to manage it, how to acquire different skills, and how to do the hard things while keeping commitments, they're going to run through walls for you.

They're going to work harder and be more engaged.

They're going to be much more invested in your company and run the extra mile for your customers — even when you're not watching.

If you truly embrace the work of the entrepreneur, you'll never be everywhere at once, and you can't always be watching. As a result, you have to put a tremendous amount of trust into the hands of your employees and the systems they run and operate. If you want your business to succeed, you need your employees to succeed.

Teaching your employees to "fish" is the only thing that makes sense if you're looking to scale your business. Find good people, give them the training to operate the systems you have built, and you'll be providing your employees — and your business — with sustenance for however long they need it. ✤

CHAPTER

21

On the Subject of Time

Michael E. Gerber

Money and time are the heaviest burdens of life and . . . the unhappiest
of all mortals are those who have more of either than they know how
to use.

—Samuel Johnson

"I'm running out of time!" contractors often lament. "I've got to
learn how to manage my time more carefully!"

Of course, they see no real solution to this problem. They're
just worrying the subject to death. Singing the contractor's blues.

Some make a real effort to control time. Maybe they go to time
management classes, or faithfully try to record their activities during
every hour of the day.

But it's hopeless. Even when these small business owners work
harder, even when they keep precise records of their time, there's
always a shortage of it. It's as if they're looking at a square clock in
a round universe. Something doesn't fit. The result: the owner of a
pest control company is constantly chasing work, money, life.

And the reason is simple. Contractors don't see time for what it
really is. They think of time with a small "t," rather than Time with
a capital "T."

Yet, Time is simply another word for *your life.* It's your ultimate asset, your gift at birth—and you can spend it any way you want. Do you know how you want to spend it? Do you have a plan?

How do *you* deal with Time? Are you even conscious of it? If you are, I bet you are constantly locked into either the future or the past. Relying on either memory or imagination.

Do you recognize these voices? "Once I get through this, I can have a drink ... go on a vacation ... retire." "I remember when I was young and the pest control business was satisfying."

As you go to bed at midnight, are you thinking about waking up at 6:00 a.m. so that you can get to the office by 7:00 a.m. so that you can get to the first house by 8:00 a.m., and you've got a full schedule and a new customer scheduled for 2:30?

Most of us are prisoners of the future or the past. While pinballing between the two, we miss the richest moments of our life—the present. Trapped forever in memory or imagination, we are strangers to the here and now. Our future is nothing more than an extension of our past, and the present is merely the background.

It's sobering to think that right now each of us is at a precise spot somewhere between the beginning of our Time (our birth) and the end of our Time (our death).

No wonder everyone frets about Time. What really terrifies us is that *we're using up our life and we can't stop it.*

It feels as if we're plummeting toward the end with nothing to break our free fall. Time is out of control! Understandably, this is horrifying, mostly because the real issue is not time with a small "t" but Death with a big "D."

From the depths of our existential anxiety, we try to put Time in a different perspective—all the while pretending we can manage it. We talk about Time as though it were something other than what it is. "Time is money," we announce, as though that explains it.

But what every pest control business owner should know is that Time is life. And Time ends! Life ends!

The big, walloping, irresolvable problem is that *we don't know how much Time we have left.*

Do you feel the fear? Do you want to get over it?

Let's look at Time more seriously.

To fully grasp Time with a capital "T," you have to ask the Big Question: *How do I wish to spend the rest of my Time?*

Because I can assure you that if you don't ask that Big Question with a big "Q," you will forever be assailed by the little questions. You'll shrink the whole of your life to *this time* and *next time* and the *last time*—all the while wondering, *what time is it?*

It's like running around the deck of a sinking ship worrying about where you left the keys to your cabin.

You must accept that you have only so much Time; that you're using up that Time second by precious second. And that your Time, your life, is the most valuable asset you have. Of course, you can use your Time any way you want. But unless you choose to use it as richly, as rewardingly, as excitingly, as intelligently, as *intentionally* as possible, you'll squander it and fail to appreciate it.

Indeed, if you are oblivious to the value of your Time, you'll commit the single greatest sin: You will live your life unconscious of its passing you by.

Until you deal with Time with a capital "T," you'll worry about time with a small "t" until you have no Time—or life—left. Then your Time will be history . . . along with your life.

I can anticipate the question: If Time is the problem, why not just take on fewer customers? Well, that's certainly an option, but probably not necessary. I know a pest control contractor with a business that sees three times as many customers as the average, yet he doesn't work long hours. How is it possible?

This contractor has a system. Roughly 50 percent of what needs to be communicated to customers is "downloaded" to the technicians and office staff. By using this expert system, the employees can do everything the owner or his managers would do—everything that isn't owner-dependent.

Be versus Do

Remember when we all asked, "What do I want to be when I grow up?" It was one of our biggest concerns as children.

Notice that the question isn't, "What do I want to *do* when I grow up?" It's "What do I want to *be?*"

Shakespeare wrote, "To be or not to be." Not "To do or not to do."

But when you grow up, people always ask you, "What do you *do?*" How did the question change from *being* to *doing?* How did we miss the critical distinction between the two?

Even as children, we sensed the distinction. The real question we were asking was not what we would end up *doing* when we grew up, but who we would *be*.

We were talking about a *life* choice, not a *work* choice. We instinctively saw it as a matter of how we spend our Time, not what we do *in* time.

Look to children for guidance. I believe that as children we instinctively saw Time as life and tried to use it wisely. As children, we wanted to make a life choice, not a work choice. As children, we didn't know—or care—that work had to be done on time, on budget.

Until you see Time for what it really is—your life span—you will always ask the wrong question.

Until you embrace the whole of your Time and shape it accordingly, you will never be able to fully appreciate the moment.

Until you fully appreciate every second that comprises Time, you will never be sufficiently motivated to live those seconds fully.

Until you're sufficiently motivated to live those seconds fully, you will never see fit to change the way you are. You will never take the quality and sanctity of Time seriously.

And unless you take the sanctity of Time seriously, you will continue to struggle to catch up with something behind you. Your frustrations will mount as you try to snatch the second that just whisked by.

If you constantly fret about time with a small "t," then big-"T" Time will blow right past you. And you'll miss the whole point, the real truth about Time: You can't manage it; you never could. You can only *live* it.

And so that leaves you with these questions: How do I live my life? How do I give significance to it? How can I be here now, in this moment?

Once you begin to ask these questions, you'll find yourself moving toward a much fuller, richer life. But if you continue to be caught up in the banal work you do every day, you're never going to find the time to take a deep breath, exhale, and be present in the now.

So let's talk about the subject of *work*. But first, let's read what Austin has to say about *time*. ✣

Making More Time

Austin Clark

"Time is the coin of your life. It is the only coin you have, and only you can determine how it will be spent. Be careful lest you let other people spend it for you."

—Carl Sandburg

Michael's description about time is some pretty deep stuff, isn't it? The truth is though, nobody talks to business owners about time like that.

Look in your inbox, or in *Pest World*, or *Pest Management Professional*. The marketing for our industry is filled with ideas and "hacks' ' to be more efficient, but surprisingly little about what to do with the time you save with that efficiency.

Of course, the marketing implies that with those precious minutes and hours you save, you should go and get another client.

Friend, let me tell you this right now: Your life is bigger than killing bugs, and so is your job.

From the very first chapter of this book, I've stated how important your life must be, and that your pest control business is not – and cannot – be the sum of your life. In many ways though, we allow ourselves to be caught up in our business, and we use our poor time management as an excuse.

I've already shared many things we've changed in our business to create more time for me as an entrepreneur, and how I've offloaded or automated a huge volume of tasks and responsibilities to my team, using systems and processes.

In doing so, I've also created *time.*

Time to give feedback and coach my team.

Time to build a system for acquiring other pest control companies around the country.

Time to enjoy a far higher quality of life with my family.

Now, you might be thinking, "Well, Austin, that's great, but I don't have that luxury! I don't have the time to learn how to make time!"

Of course you do, but you have to make the conscious decision to change your business to change your time.

Do What You're Good At

The first rule of time, for me, is the simplest – do what you're good at. In my own life, that's sales. Sure, I can handle fieldwork, and I can do the paperwork associated with our business, but it's not because I'm a natural at it.

In fact, if I had to go to a client's house today, I'd literally have to look at our training systems to ensure I did it properly! The same holds true for any of our internal office systems. You might think that's funny, or even pathetic, but it's the truth. The systems we used when I was doing field work and administrative tasks have changed dramatically (for the better!), and I'm blessed to have a team following those systems.

…And while you might think that shows I don't know how to do the work in my own company, in reality, it's exactly the way it should be for an entrepreneur. I helped create the systems, I helped create the way those systems are managed and innovated, and I helped hire and train the men and women who actually run them.

As an owner and a managing partner, it's not the best use of my time to try to do that work. We've got far better people for that.

Does that mean you, as the owner of a small pest control company, aren't "worthy" of this type of leadership role?

Not at all.

But again and again, I see these small business owners who try to keep their entire business in their mind. They can't – or won't – document it, and the results are simple: a business that cannot scale because these owners can't make enough time.

The truth of the matter is, you've got all the answers to your growth problems, you just can't see them for all the "busy-ness" you're dealing with.

For all the time you're allowing yourself to waste.

The point of this chapter isn't to simply restate the countless tactics Michael and I have already shared. It's about understanding that right now, you are somewhere between birth and death, and to the degree you choose to be active in how your time each day is spent, that's the degree to which you'll be able to not only "have" more time, but you'll be able to enjoy more of that time.

While I encourage you to "do what you're good at," I also have to encourage you to actively grow – both as an entrepreneur and as a person. Your job description in a year can't be the same as it was this year, just as your personal skills and hobbies should improve as you use and enjoy them.

Think of a professional athlete – let's say Michael Jordan. He's arguably the best basketball player ever, and if you analyze his growth as a player, you begin to see he didn't play the game the same way towards the end of his career as he did as a rookie.

Yes, he was still great, but that greatness *evolved*. He was technically proficient, but his leadership skills had grown.

His greatness had matured.

It's really no different with our industry – think about it: how did you manage to make that first sale all those years ago? How did you feel as a young technician going into people's homes for the first time?

You probably don't think about it anymore because, "just like Mike," you've matured.

And your time and your life are more than that. It's time to look beyond simply being an efficient or experienced technician and move into the realm of using time, not experience, in a more efficient way to allow you to grow as a business owner.

It's time to truly be an entrepreneur.

Controlling Your Time

The key takeaway I want you to have from this chapter is simple: to become an entrepreneur, your focus must shift to making time, not just money.

As we've seen, the core of this idea is using systems and processes to manage your company, and also, identifying the tasks that you, as a leader and CEO, should not be doing, or should be actively working on offloading to others.

These are the technical and managerial jobs within your business.

They're also the jobs you especially dislike.

Let me explain.

I've never met a pest control owner who likes doing office work. Given the choice between the most disgusting work out in the field our industry offers – bedbugs, cockroach nests, *anything* in crawlspaces – most of us would charge off into the field instead of reconciling our cashflow statements.

Here's the cool thing about being an entrepreneur: you don't HAVE to do either.

Hire it out!

I know what you're thinking, and you're wrong, "Austin, I can't afford to hire that type of stuff out! I'm still using a free copy of QuickBooks to run my company!"

You've got to change that way of thinking. Instead of saying "I/we can't afford that!" change your thoughts to, "How can I/we afford that?"

That's how you not only make more time, but it's also how you ensure the time you make is quality time instead of simply replacing one task for another.

Many pest control owners don't allow themselves to think their time spent working can really be "quality" time – that's supposed to be reserved for vacations, or family, or some mythical retirement goal they'll struggle to achieve.

I maintain that your business should provide you with enjoyment. Sure, Jordan played a sport and became wealthy, but the fact he enjoyed it surely made it easier for him to want to continue to do it. Why can't your business be any different?

People need the services we provide, and most of us get a real feeling of satisfaction from providing a solution to each client. Think about a client you've sorted out a big problem for – it felt good to leave their house or their office, didn't it?

Now imagine creating a system that could do that ten times a day. Or twenty.

Or one thousand!

The truth is, I can't write a chapter about "time" without acknowledging the fact that you're managing time right now, whether you like it or not. Throughout this book, Michael and I are giving you a lot of ways you can manage time differently, and in ways that will provide you, your employees, and your customers with a far bigger result than you might ever have thought possible.

It all comes back to your decision – every day – about how you'll manage time.

The 86,400 Second Decision

When Michael and I talk about time, it's easy to get overwhelmed by it, but it really comes down to how you choose to manage the 86,400 seconds you've got in a day. By reading this book, you've probably got some ideas on what tasks you might like to automate, and maybe what systems you should address first, so let's spend a few minutes discussing how you actually build that system.

Any way you cut it, to make more time, just like money, you have to spend some time. To begin with, it really doesn't matter whether it's a task you do, or a part of your team's daily ritual.

You document it, or you ask them to.

Step by step by step.

The "why" doesn't really matter, the steps do, at this point. That's part of innovating and optimizing the system once it's down on paper. You might end up with forty steps in this process, or it might be ten.

It might be how your team answers the phone, it might be how they meet a new single family home client for termite services, or it might be how your entire company processes payments automatically in the field.

Step by step.

Analyze it, adjust it, and relaunch it.

System by system.

Each one goes into your operations manuals, in the proper category.

Yes, this takes time to create, and time to document, and time to refine.

Guess what?

It takes time to do the way you're doing it now!

Time you're wasting, time you're paying for, time that is keeping your company from growing, time that is adding to the stress you feel each day, each week, each month, and each year.

…And time that's being robbed from you for living and enjoying your life.

The decisions you make – or don't make – about how you'll conduct and operate your pest control business will impact the satisfaction you take from it – day to day, week to week, and over the entire course of your ownership.

You have the power to decide if it will be a fun journey, one filled with growth and profit, or if it will be a tedious, mind-numbing job that will rob you of your youth and your enjoyment.

Spend your time wisely. ✤

CHAPTER

23

On the Subject of Work

Michael E. Gerber

They intoxicate themselves with work so they don't see how they really are.

—Aldous Huxley

In the business world, as the saying goes, the entrepreneur knows something about everything, the technician knows everything about something, and the switchboard operator just knows everything.

In a pest control business, owners see their natural work as the work of the technician. The Supreme Technician. Often to the exclusion of everything else.

After all, these owners have gotten zero preparation working as a manager and spend no time thinking as an entrepreneur—those just aren't courses offered in today's trade schools or industry certifications. By the time they have their own pest control business, they're just doing it, doing it, doing it.

At the same time, they want everything—freedom, respect, money. Most of all, they want to rid themselves of meddling bosses and start their own business. That way they can be their own boss and take home all the money. These contractors are in the throes of an entrepreneurial seizure.

Contractors who have been praised for their amazing skills believe they have what it takes to run their own pest control company. It's not unlike the plumber who becomes a contractor because he's a great plumber. Sure, he may be a great plumber . . . but it doesn't necessarily follow that he knows how to build a business that does this work.

It's the same for a pest control contractor. So many of them are surprised to wake up one morning and discover that they're nowhere near as equipped for owning their own business as they thought they were.

More than any other subject, work is the cause of obsessive-compulsive behavior by contractors.

Work. You've got to do it every single day.

Work. If you fall behind, you'll pay for it.

Work. There's either too much or not enough.

So many contractors describe work as what they do when they're busy. Some discriminate between the work they *could* be doing as contractors and the work they *should* be doing as contractors.

But according to the E-Myth, they're exactly the same thing. The work you *could* do and the work you *should* do as the owner of a pest control business is identical. Let me explain.

Strategic Work versus Tactical Work

Contractors can do only two kinds of work: strategic work and tactical work.

Tactical work is easier to understand, because it's what almost every contractor does almost every minute of every hour of every day. It's called getting the job done. It's called doing business.

Tactical work includes servicing, installing, inspecting, customer education, managing subs, marketing, filing, billing, bookkeeping, dictating letters, quoting jobs, returning calls, going to the bank, and seeing customers.

The E-Myth says that tactical work is all the work contractors find themselves doing in a pest control business to *avoid* doing the strategic work.

"I'm too busy," most of these owners will tell you.

"How come nothing goes right unless I do it myself?" they complain in frustration.

Owners say these things when they're up to their ears in tactical work. But most owners don't understand that if they had done more strategic work, they would have less tactical work to do.

These same men and women are doing strategic work when they ask the following questions:

- Why do I own a pest control business?
- What will my business look like when it's done?
- What must my business look, act, and feel like in order for it to compete successfully?
- What are the key indicators of my business?

Please note that I said owners *ask* these questions when they are doing strategic work. I didn't say these are the questions they necessarily answer.

That is the fundamental difference between strategic work and tactical work. Tactical work is all about *answers*: How to do this. How to do that.

Strategic work, in contrast, is all about *questions*: What business are we really in? Why are we in that business? Who specifically is our business determined to serve? When will I sell this business? How and where will this business be doing business when I sell it? And so forth.

Not that strategic questions don't have answers. Owners who commonly ask strategic questions know that once they ask such a question, they're already on their way to *envisioning* the answer. Question and answer are part of a whole. You can't find the right answer until you've asked the right question.

Tactical work is much easier, because the question is always more obvious. In fact, you don't ask the tactical question; instead, the question arises from a result you need to get or from a problem you need to solve. Billing a customer is tactical work. Spraying a house or a yard is tactical work. Firing an employee is tactical work. Setting up glue traps in a hot attic or damp crawlspace is tactical work.

Tactical work is the stuff you do every day in your business. Strategic work is the stuff you plan to do to create an exceptional sole proprietorship / business / enterprise.

In tactical work, the question comes from *out there* rather than *in here*. The tactical question is about something *outside* of you, whereas the strategic question is about something *inside* of you.

The tactical question is about something you *need* to do, whereas the strategic question is about something you *want* to do. Want versus need.

If tactical work consumes you,

- you are always reacting to something outside of you;
- your business runs you; you don't run it;
- your employees run you; you don't run them; and
- your life runs you; you don't run your life.

You must understand that the more strategic work you do, the more intentional your decisions, your business, and your life become. *Intention* is the byword of strategic work.

Everything on the outside begins to serve you, to serve your vision, rather than forcing you to serve it. Everything you *need* to do is congruent with *what* you want to do. It means you have a vision, an aim, a purpose, a strategy, an *envisioned* result.

Strategic work is the work you do to *design* your business, to design your life.

Tactical work is the work you do to *implement* the design created by strategic work.

Without strategic work, there is no design. Without strategic work, all that's left is keeping busy.

There's only one thing left to do. It's time to take *action*.

But first, let's read what Austin has to say about *work*. ✤

It Isn't Always Work

Austin Clark

"Working hard and working smart sometimes can be two different things."

—Byron Dorgan

As I've shared already, one of the primary growth tools we use now is acquisition. For several years, we've bought or partnered with smaller pest control companies all over the United States, and that's been very enlightening when it comes to the idea of *work*.

I speak with scores of pest control company owners, and nearly all of them are incredibly hard workers.

They've built their company from the ground up or went to work in a business started by their dad, or grandfather, or an uncle, and they know how to do every single job in it. These men and women work voraciously!

Usually, by the time I get to meet them, they've learned some hard facts – mainly, if they don't do it, it doesn't get done. And no matter how big their company is, they're so intertwined in its operation, they'll never be able to take a few days off without a significant amount of "work" waiting on them when they come back.

Even if they're not the ones handling the actual field work (which they often still are), they will have to deal with a laundry list of items on a nearly daily basis:

- Marketing problems
- A/R problems
- Human resources issues
- Staffing problems
- Supply chain demands

As Michael pointed out, in the end all of these are tactical issues, and the problem with tactical issues, for most owners, is they've never learned how to systemize the tactical work in their pest control business so they aren't the ones doing it.

In fact, many of the owners I speak with proudly share their own stories of growth and expansion, and when I press them, what they've really done is simply add enough systems to their business to allow them to become managers.

In other words, they're still doing tactical work, but it's in an office now. The problems that affected them – exchanging time for money – still affect them.

I've made more than a few of them angry when I've pointed out they could have a far better quality of life if they simply took a job as a manager for a bigger pest control company, because that's what they're doing right now – but with all the extra stress of being the owner.

Becoming Truly Strategic

In a lot of ways, my own experience in the pest control industry was a real gift. Maybe it was because my background was from the sales side of things and not the technical roles in the field or the office. The work, as I always have understood it, simply didn't seem to be that hard.

Sure, you have to know what chemicals are safe and effective, you have to know your customers, and you have to have a process in place to be successful, but it all seemed very matter-of-fact to me. To put it simply, I didn't know what I didn't know, and as it came time to create a position, or design a process, or build a management system, I never thought I was smart enough, or "experienced" enough to be able to do it on the tactical level.

When I'd begin to focus on these things, I'd often find that there wasn't any real magic to doing the job IF there was a process in place.

Here's where the problems start: business owners don't place a value on their own time – it's simply work that has to get done. They fall back on their technical experience and just jump right in, doing it, doing it, doing it.

What I'm challenging you, as a reader and an entrepreneur, to do is this: quit using your own time, labor, and skillset to handle everything. Change that thinking, and learn how to use money, planning, management, people, clients, systems, and this book to STOP focusing on every problem and challenge being yours to solve and instead, focus on the core mission and values of your business.

Yes, I'll admit, this might have been an easier step for me in some respects, since I never thought of myself as a skilled technician in the field. I knew what needed to be done, but I'd never had to develop the skills to be the best technician in the company. Essentially, this made me ask questions, determine metrics, and learn how to change and innovate the processes we'd developed.

In other words, it opened up a whole range of possibilities that others with different experiences might not have looked into. Here's the good news though: just like you can teach someone to do the technical work of the job, you can teach *yourself* to do the strategic work of the entrepreneur.

Growing Into Strategic Work

Think back to when you learned the pest control business. There are basically two ways most owners learned it: they went to work for a big national name as technicians, and then, at some point, decided to open their own business (what Michael would call an "entrepreneurial seizure"), or they sort of fell into a family-run business by birth or by accident.

In either example, they could have learned their job from shadowing another technician, a more in-depth training system, or, in some cases, especially with the chemicals we use in our industry, it might even have been a third-party course.

In any case, the focus wasn't on customer service, or billing, or ordering, or scheduling.

It was about safety and doing The Job. The technical field-based work of pest control. Period.

Obviously, that's a problem, because in the blue-collar world, many of us have been conditioned to believe the longer we've done the technical work of the business, The Job, the more highly skilled they are.

Not at all. Years of working in the pest control business, or any other business, really only means that person *might* be more *efficient* in doing the work. Efficiency in action is not, and cannot, be the key to becoming an entrepreneur. It certainly can help you to create extra time to work on your business, and it will allow you to make more money, but efficiency alone will do little for you.

You've got to *re*think how you *think*.

All that "field" and "technical" experience you have is really only allowing you to exchange time for money faster. The real "work" you have to do isn't the "work" you've been conditioned to think about.

I've never heard anyone in a training class on pest control discuss hiring basics for your administrative team. I've never read any articles in our industry periodicals about the relative merits of cash versus accrual-based accounting, or been on a webinar for pest control professionals where the host was sharing the importance of building a company based on your dream, vision, purpose, and mission.

The strategic work I'm asking you to do now isn't about making you better at "pest control" or more efficient, it's about rethinking the business you've built.

Imagine building a pest control business that serves your dreams? One that cultivates your business skills? A business that allows you to be paid for your mind instead of your labor? Leverage your experience into systems that can run your business for you, then use your motivation to learn the real skills of entrepreneurship in the strategic realm. ❧

On the Subject of Taking Action

Michael E. Gerber

You should know now that a man of knowledge lives by acting, not by thinking about acting, nor by thinking about what he will think when he has finished acting. A man of knowledge chooses a path with heart and follows it.

—Carlos Castaneda, *A Separate Reality*

It's time to get started, time to take action. Time to stop thinking about the old sole proprietorship and start thinking about the new business. It's not a matter of coming up with better businesses; it's about reinventing the business of pest control.

And the owner has to take personal responsibility for it.

That's you.

So sit up and pay attention!

You, the owner, have to be interested. You cannot abdicate accountability for the business of pest control, the administration of pest control, or the finance of pest control.

Although the goal is to create systems into which you, as an owner, can plug reasonably competent people—systems that allow the business to run without them—owners must take responsibility for that happening.

I can hear the chorus now: "But we're just the "bug guys!" We shouldn't have to know about this." To that I say: whatever. If you don't give a flip about your business, fine—close your mind to new knowledge and accountability. But if you want to succeed, then you'd better step up and take responsibility, and you'd better do it now.

All too often, contractors take no responsibility for the business of pest control but instead delegate tasks without any understanding of what it takes to do them; without any interest in what their people are actually doing; without any sense of what it feels like to be at the job site when a customer is kept waiting for a technician for four hours; and without any appreciation for the entity that is creating their livelihood.

As a business owner, you can open the portals of change in an instant. All you have to do is say, "I don't want to do it that way anymore." Saying it will begin to set you free—even though you don't yet understand what the business will look like after it's been reinvented.

This demands an intentional leap from the known into the unknown. It further demands that you live there—in the unknown—for a while. It means discarding the past, everything you once believed to be true.

Think of it as soaring rather than plunging.

Thought Control

You should now be clear about the need to organize your thoughts first, then your business. Because the organization of your thoughts is the foundation for the organization of your business.

If we try to organize our business without organizing our thoughts, we will fail to attack the problem.

We have seen that organization is not simply time management. Nor is it people management. Nor is it tidying up desks or alphabetizing customer files. Organization is first, last, and always cleaning up the mess of our minds.

By learning how to *think* about the business of pest control, by learning how to *think* about your priorities, and by learning how to *think* about your life, you'll prepare yourself to do righteous battle with the forces of failure.

Right thinking leads to right action—and now is the time to take action. Because it is only through action that you can translate thoughts into movement in the real world, and, in the process, find fulfillment.

So, first, *think* about what you want to do. Then *do* it. Only in this way will you be fulfilled.

How do you put the principles we've discussed in this book to work in your pest control business? To find out, accompany me down the path once more:

1. *Create a story about your company.* Your story should be an idealized version of your pest control company, a vision of what the pre-eminent leader in your field should be and why. Your story must become the very heart of your business. It must become the spirit that mobilizes it, as well as everyone who walks through the doors. Without this story, your business will be reduced to plain work.

2. *Organize your company so that it breathes life into your story.* Unless your company can faithfully replicate your story in action, it all becomes fiction. In that case, you'd be better off not telling your story at all. And without a story, you'd be better off leaving your business the way it is and just hoping for the best.

Here are some tips for organizing your pest control company:

*   Identify the key functions of your business.
*   Identify the essential processes that link those functions.

- Identify the results you have determined your company will produce.
- Clearly state in writing how each phase will work.

Take it step by step. Think of your business as a program, a piece of software, a system. It is a collaboration, a collection of processes dynamically interacting with one another.

Of course, your business is also people.

3. *Engage your people in the process.* Why is this the third step rather than the first? Because, contrary to the advice most business experts will give you, you must never engage your people in the process until you yourself are clear about what you intend to do.

The need for consensus is a disease of today's addled mind. It's a product of our troubled and confused times. When people don't know what to believe in, they often ask others to tell them. To ask is not to lead but to follow.

The prerequisite of sound leadership is first to know where you wish to go.

And so, "What do *I* want?" becomes the first question; not, "What do *they* want?" In your own business, the vision must first be yours. To follow another's vision is to abdicate your personal accountability, your leadership role, your true power.

In short, the role of leader cannot be delegated or shared. And without leadership, no pest control business will ever succeed.

Despite what you have been told, *win-win* is a secondary step, not a primary one. The opposite of *win-win* is not necessarily *they lose*.

Let's say "they" can win by choosing a good horse. The best choice will not be made by consensus. "Guys, what horse do you think we should ride?" will always lead to endless and worthless discussions. By the time you're done jawing, the horse will have already left the post.

Before you talk to your people about what you intend to do in your business and why you intend to do it, you need to reach agreement with yourself.

It's important to know (1) *exactly* what you want, (2) how you intend to proceed, (3) what's important to you and what isn't, and (4) what you want the business to be and how you want it to get there.

Once you have that agreement, it's critical that you engage your people in a discussion about what you intend to do and why. Be clear—both with yourself and with them.

The Story

The story is paramount because it is your vision. Tell it with passion and conviction. Tell it with precision. Never hurry a great story. Unveil it slowly. Don't mumble or show embarrassment. Never apologize or display false modesty. Look your audience in the eyes and tell your story as though it is the most important one they'll ever hear about business. Your business. The company into which you intend to pour your heart, your soul, your intelligence, your imagination, your time, your money, and your sweaty persistence.

Get into the storytelling zone. Behave as though it means everything to you. Show no equivocation when telling your story.

These tips are important because you're going to tell your story over and over—to customers, to new and old employees, to contractors, to subcontractors, to technicians, and to your family and friends. You're going to tell it at your church or synagogue, to your card-playing or fishing buddies, and to organizations such as Kiwanis, Rotary, YMCA, Hadassah, and the Boy Scouts.

There are few moments in your life when telling a great story about a great company is inappropriate.

If it is to be persuasive, you must love your story. Do you think Walt Disney loved his Disneyland story? Or Ray Kroc his McDonald's story? What about Fred Smith at Federal Express? Or Debbi Fields at Mrs. Fields Cookies? Or Tom Watson Jr. at IBM?

Do you think these people loved their stories? Do you think others loved (and *still* love) to hear them? I daresay *all* successful entrepreneurs have loved the story of their business. Because that's what true entrepreneurs do. They tell stories that come to life in the form of their business.

Remember: A great story never fails. A great story is always a joy to hear.

In summary, you first need to clarify, both for yourself and for your people, the *story* of your business. Then you need to detail the *process* your business must go through to make your story become reality.

I call this the business development process. Others call it re-engineering, continuous improvement, reinventing your business, or total quality management.

Whatever you call it, you must take three distinct steps to succeed:

1. *Innovation.* Continue to find better ways of doing what you do.
2. *Quantification.* Once that is achieved, quantify the impact of these improvements on your business.
3. *Orchestration.* Once these improvements are verified, orchestrate this better way of running your business so that it becomes your standard, to be repeated time and again.

In this way, the system works—no matter who's using it. And you've built a business that works consistently, predictably, systematically. A business you can depend on to operate exactly as promised, every single time.

Your vision, your people, your process—all linked.

A superior pest control business is a creation of your imagination, a product of your mind. So fire it up and get started! Now let's read what Austin has to say about *taking action.* ❧

Taking *Purposeful* Action

Austin Clark

"The key to success is action, and the essential in action is perseverance."

—Sun Yat-sen

For most of the owners of smaller pest control companies, the problem with taking strategic, or purposeful, action is focus.

You might be motivated to take action, but you're so "busy" doing other things it's hard to get any real traction.

I'm not talking about things that aren't important either.

You've got to be a parent, or a spouse, or handle some technical work in your company, or even some seemingly important strategic work in your business.

...But creating real change is *very* hard.

Let me give you an example, but one that's personal, not professional...

It started with a broken taillight. I was pulled over, but the police officer decided to take mercy on me. He gave me a fix-it ticket instead of a normal ticket. Basically, I was allowed to go on about my business under the assumption I would fix it by the time the court date came around, and then I'd avoid paying any type of fine. Then, once you've fixed the problem, you just fill out a form to inform your city or state that you've made the change.

Even though I'd gotten the taillight fixed immediately, I put off filling out the form.

I went back to being a father, a husband, and an entrepreneur. Unfortunately, since the city didn't know I'd fixed the taillight, they started sending me notices. These went something along the lines of: "Hey, friendly reminder, you are supposed to fix your vehicle by this date. If not, your license is at risk of being suspended."

This went on for six months, and unfortunately, those notices weren't going to my home or office – in fact, I have no idea where they were going – but I never received them.

Finally, after several months and numerous notices, I happened to be pulled over again, for something unrelated – it might even have been another taillight - but this time, I didn't get off so easily.

The police officer informed me my license was suspended. At the time, the state of Arizona had a regulation that required officers to impound your vehicle if they caught you driving on a suspended license — immediately.

Remember that sinking feeling I shared with you about when I had to pawn the title to Ashtyn's car? It was like that all over again. I had to call her to ask her to pick me up, we had to get the car out of impound, and I had to pay all types of fines because I had not filled out one simple form.

Just think of all the money, time, and resources I wasted, all because I had put off something that would take me five minutes to do. Even worse? Think about the time I took away from Ashtyn. I don't know what she might have had to do that day, but *my* procrastination forced my problem to become *her* problem. How many times does this happen to you in the course of running your business? This is just one of the consequences of procrastination, and it is especially dangerous for business owners.

Identify Your Habits

While I would like to say that I learned my lesson with the fix-it ticket and that I never procrastinate anymore — I can't. Even in the office, I catch myself avoiding tasks more than I'd like to admit. The worst part is the ease at which I can rationalize it! I find myself scrolling our internal communication platforms whenever I'm avoiding work … it might be slack, email, or my team's updates and messages … much more frequently than I should. I KNOW it's completely unnecessary – if there's an actual emergency, there are better ways to contact me, and an entire system is in place if something really bad occurs.

Another one of my time-wasting defaults is spending hours in the warehouse of our Phoenix office. If I'm ever putting off some work, I'll head back there and start organizing our products or taking the trash out — any activity that doesn't take too much brainpower.

Remember when I shared the simple idea of assigning a value to every task you do?

Taking out the trash or organizing our chemical room isn't where I serve my team or our clients.

Sure, "it needs to be done…"

…Just not by me. And, just like an emergency, we've got processes to ensure the trash is taken out and the chemicals are organized.

If you're a business owner, you probably have your own go-to procrastination activity. While that isn't necessarily a bad thing, it can be valuable to identify these defaults so you can effectively avoid them.

Own the fact you're wasting time and take a moment to say, "I'm procrastinating right now. Stop." The first step in breaking or redirecting a bad habit is to be aware of when you're doing it. If you identify the problem, you can work on the solution.

Now, if you're like me and struggle with completing some tasks, then I have a little exercise for you to try that I picked up from Stephen Covey's book, *The 7 Habits of Highly Effective People*.

Visualize your funeral service.

Morbid? Sure, but it's also one of the only absolutes in our lives. What do you want others to say about you when you die?

What impression do you want to leave – on your family, in your industry, and in the world?

Here's a hint – until you decide what you truly want to do, the impression you leave is liable to be far smaller than you might want. The first time I actually did this exercise, I was able to zero in on the things that were most important to me. It helped me identify my core values and write my personal mission statement, and understand how I could create a far bigger impact in the world through the work our company does.

It also made it clear to me how I wanted us to conduct our business, how I wanted us to be viewed by customers, team members, and even the suppliers and vendors we used.

When I began to gain clarity on my personal and professional vision, it was far easier to sit down and do the tasks that were essential for achieving my vision.

Did this make me perfect? Not at all. But it helped me identify goals that were bigger than family or finance, and to this day, it allows me to stay on track. Today, it's rare for me not to be up by 4:00 a.m., but I'm not working, I'm taking time for me, personally. I'm not scrolling social media, but I might be studying a business book, exercising or meditating.

Determining What's Important

I can't tell you how valuable it is to have this kind of personal and professional vision. As I clarified it, I could reverse-engineer what needed to be done to ensure the business could reach the goals I set for it.

If you think about it, and you take the strategic view of the entrepreneur, it's suddenly easy to see what $1,000/hour things you need to work on to meet the vision you have for how your business might look years from now at your funeral.

If you want to create a pest control company that's still succeeding in fifty years, ask yourself what you need to be doing today to make that vision a reality.

These are what I call important, but not urgent, tasks.

As business owners, many of us spend time on tasks that are urgent but not important. These are things like text messages, phone calls, and emails — tasks that aren't planned and take time away from your more important projects.

Unfortunately, it can be extremely difficult to stay focused on your tasks that are important but not urgent. They're easy to put off while you're busy taking care of what seems more critical at the moment.

It's the trap Michael has warned us about for over forty years! Working IN your business and not ON your business. Working *in* your business means you're not *developing* your business.

You're stagnant.

I've already mentioned how our growth today focuses on acquisitions, and I can't tell you the number of small pest control companies I speak to who have been in operation for decades and still struggle financially. There are plenty of reasons for this, but ultimately, it comes down to the actions these owners decide to take in their business, day after day.

I'll be blunt: It hurts me to speak with a person who has owned a pest control business for thirty years and still struggles to hit $500,000 annually. Our industry has literally given me everything I have, and when I see others fighting to keep the doors open, or to make a decent living, it bothers me. Especially when, with some focus and some attention, that same business could be creating life-changing income.

In all honesty, it took me far longer than I'd like to admit to really begin to focus on the truly important work of the entrepreneur, too. Even now, the best way I've found to avoid procrastinating on these projects is to schedule them in my calendar every quarter.

I can't avoid them, and I can't forget them, and I can make and manage my time to address them. Today I'm proud to say I now plan everything else - including those more urgent tasks - around these critical items. I simply have no excuse for not accomplishing my mission.

Action Versus Purposeful Action

One of the facts you're going to have to confront in your pest control business is that all actions are not created equally.

Let me explain it this way: Have you ever gone fishing? If so, how many fish did you catch while you were buying your fishing license? Probably zero. How many did you catch while you were buying the hooks and fishing line and bait? I'm guessing your answer is still zero. What about when you were driving to the lake or river, or finding the perfect spot to cast your line? Unless a fish jumped into your pocket, I imagine your answer remains the same: zero.

Ultimately, the only chance you have of actually catching a fish is when you cast your line and bait into the water. Even then, there is no guarantee you will catch something.

You can't confuse activities that support fishing with actually fishing. If you ever want to catch a fish, you have to be fishing, not just doing fishing things.

Where do I see a lot of pest control business owners making mistakes? They miss the real purpose of the actions they should be taking.

They want to bring in leads, so they spend their time marketing.

They want to close sales, so they spend their time selling.

They want to hire great people, so they spend their time hiring.

Here's the problem: as an entrepreneur, your real job isn't – to go back to our earlier example - catching fish.

It's not killing bugs, or treating for termites, or worrying about snakes in a crawlspace.

Your job, as the owner, is *growing the business*. That growth is the result of taking purposeful action, such as: creating the systems to ensure great hires. That ensure closed sales. That ensure lead generation. That ensure fishing licenses get purchased. And hooks baited. And lines cast. And so on…

In reality, your role as an entrepreneur is no longer static. You're not a technician. You're not a manager. You're not, as a rule, following a specific job description.

Frankly, you're not the person "fishing" anymore.

You're an entrepreneur who owns a pest control business. You isolate a job or a task that is to be systemized, you document how it should operate, you create a plan to hire the right person for it, and then, you create a training system to teach them how to do it.

Purposeful action means you have spent the time to create a system that teaches your team *exactly* how to buy the fishing license, *exactly* how to bait the hook, *exactly* how to drive to the lake, and even, *exactly* how to catch the fish.

The role of the entrepreneur is teaching someone else to fish. To buy the license. To read the map. To cast the line.

Over and over and over again.

You're a teacher, and your pest control business is the school.

You might be thinking, "But Austin, I really like doing the technical work! Why can't I continue to do field work?"

To be blunt – and completely honest – you can.

But if you decide to do that, give this book to someone who will truly utilize the information in it, because if you choose to continue to do "the job" – the technical work of our industry – then you've made the active decision to allow your business to simply stay small.

Call my team, because you might as well sell your company and go to work for someone else. You'll probably make more money, almost surely work fewer hours, and your quality of life will surely improve. I don't mean to offend you, but if you're not willing to make changes in your business, then you'll continue to get what you've always gotten – and that's almost certainly not enough.

Seriously – you picked up this book for a reason, and that reason was to improve your business, right?

You'll only do it if you commit to taking purposeful action.

Anything else is just the status quo…

Perfection is Poverty

If you're still reading, and you didn't launch this book across the room, great!

Now, I can't tell you exactly how to start taking purposeful action, but I can tell you that you'll learn much more if you're actually doing *something*.

It may not be perfect, and you may make mistakes, but you'll learn and grow so much quicker than if you spend all your time planning, waiting, and procrastinating. Pick a place in the business – and begin to build and refine how that work is actually done.

You might build a flowchart, you might simply write a list with bullet points.

Anything is better than nothing, and as you take action, you'll also learn where things are broken. If you've got an office manager, ask them what they do, and ask them to explain it.

Don't be afraid to ask questions, or to wonder aloud why your company has to do things *this* way versus *that* way.

For example, we've been moving toward a monthly subscription model over the past couple of years, the whole industry has. We did this because we had scaled to multiple service offerings but didn't have an effective pricing model to match.

In other words, we were offering general pest control — spiders, scorpions, things of that nature - and had a set cost for those services. At the same time, we were also offering weeds, termites, and specialty work like bees and bedbugs. Those jobs were priced a la carte: X amount of dollars for weeds, X amount for termites, and so on. It was an inconvenient process, for both our customers and our team.

On the other hand, with a subscription model, our customers could choose whatever type of service they wanted to be covered, and we would give them a set price to pay each month.

We got to work putting this subscription model together. After about two or three months, we had it about 90% complete. It would've been easy to keep tweaking and perfecting it, but I knew that the time had come to push it out to our customers. We had beat it to death, and if I kept procrastinating, I knew I might never finish it.

I also knew that once I released it to our customers, we would learn very, very quickly what still needed to be fixed.

And that's exactly what happened. We sent it out, and our clients shared their feedback. There were some mistakes, but we were able to fix them and build something that works better for everyone.

If you're worried about taking action and releasing something that doesn't feel perfect, my advice is this: just do it.

Think of companies like Apple or Android. I currently have an iPhone, and it seems like every ten days there's a new update. That's because they're always working on eliminating bugs — no pun intended.

Do you think Apple waits for their updates to be perfect before they release them? No way. They know that their users will give them feedback, and they might as well make a buck along the way.

Do you want to plan?

Yes.

Do you want to take calculated risks?

Of course.

Do you want to do right by your customers?

Absolutely, every single time.

Eventually though, there comes a point when you just have to get out there and do it.

So here is my challenge to you: start taking action, even if it's a risk. Don't do anything stupid - like forgetting to pay your fix-it ticket - but try pushing out a new service or product that's not quite done yet. What's the worst that could happen? Chances are, you'll get great feedback from your customers and be able to improve your business on a quicker timeline with better results.

If you fail, you'll fail fast, and you'll be able to get back up again, and make an improvement. No matter what you do, keep moving forward! ✤

AFTERWORD

Michael E. Gerber

For more than three decades, I've applied the E-Myth principles I've shared with you in this book to the successful development of thousands of small businesses throughout the world. Many have been contracting businesses—with contractors specializing in everything from pest control to residential remodeling to commercial developing.

Few rewards are greater than seeing these E-Myth principles improve the work and lives of so many people. Those rewards include seeing these changes:

- Lack of clarity—clarified
- Lack of organization—organized
- Lack of direction—shaped into a path that is clearly, lovingly, passionately pursued
- Lack of money or money poorly managed—money understood instead of coveted; created instead of chased; wisely spent or invested instead of squandered
- Lack of committed people—transformed into a cohesive community working in harmony toward a common goal; discovering each other and themselves in the process; all the while expanding their understanding, their know-how, their interest, their attention

After working with so many contractors, I know that a business can be much more than what most become. I also know that nothing is preventing you from making your pest control business all that it can be. It takes only desire and the perseverance to see it through.

In this book—the next of its kind in the E-Myth Expert series—the E-Myth principles have been complemented and enriched by stories from Austin Clark, a real-life pest control *entrepreneur* who has put these principles to use in his pest control business. Austin had the desire and perseverance to achieve success beyond his wildest dreams. Now you, too, can join his ranks.

I hope this book has helped you clear your vision and set your sights on a very bright future.

To your business!

ABOUT THE AUTHORS

Michael E. Gerber

Michael E. Gerber is the legend behind the E-Myth series of books, which includes The E-Myth Revisited, E-Myth Mastery, The E-Myth Manager, The E-Myth Enterprise, Awakening the Entrepreneur Within, and Beyond The E-Myth. Collectively, his books have sold millions of copies worldwide. He is the founder of In the Dreaming Room™, a process to awaken the entrepreneur within, Origination™, which trains facilitators to assist entrepreneurs in growing "turnkey" businesses, and Radical U™, the only online entrepreneurial trade school of its kind. Michael E. Gerber is chairman of the Michael E. Gerber Companies. A highly sought-after speaker and consultant, he has trained more than 70,000 businesses in his career. Michael lives with his wife, Luz Delia, in Carlsbad, California.

ABOUT THE CO-AUTHOR

Austin Clark

Austin Clark is the CEO of Moxie Pest Control of Arizona and has been a driving force in rethinking the traditional business model many pest control companies have used for decades. His innovative ideas for both growth and operations have resulted in double- and triple-digit growth in his markets. More importantly, his commitment to the ideas of Michael E. Gerber's *E-Myth Revisited* have helped to create a system that ANY pest control company can adopt, use, and profit from.

With over 10 years of leadership experience, and nearly two decades in the pest control industry, Austin is now sharing how smart pest control companies can "E-Myth" their own businesses and take them to the next level, developing outstanding leaders, creating a truly gifted team, and build great relationships with clients and vendors.

Austin is an Arizona native, who graduated from Arizona State with a BSBA. He currently resides in Mesa, AZ with his wife and 4 children and in his free time loves to BBQ, travel, exercise and read.

ABOUT THE SERIES

The E-Myth Expert series brings Michael E. Gerber's proven E-Myth philosophy to a wide variety of different professional business areas. The E-Myth, short for "Entrepreneurial Myth," is simple: too many small businesses fail to grow because their leaders think like technicians, not entrepreneurs. Gerber's approach gives small enterprise leaders practical, proven methods that have already helped transform more than 70,000 businesses. Let the E-Myth Expert series boost your professional business today!

Books in the series include:

The E-Myth Accountant	*The E-Myth Insurance Store*
The E-Myth Architect	*The E-Myth Landscape Contractor*
The E-Myth Attorney	*The E-Myth Nutritionist*
The E-Myth Bookkeeper	*The E-Myth Optometrist*
The E-Myth Chief Financial Officer	*The E-Myth Physician*
	The E-Myth Real Estate Agent
The E-Myth Chiropractor	*The E-Myth Real Estate Brokerage*
The E-Myth Contractor	*The E-Myth Real Estate Investor*
The E-Myth Dentist	*The E-Myth Veterinarian*
The E-Myth Financial Advisor	*. . . and 300 more industries and*
The E-Myth HVAC Contractor	*professions*

Forthcoming books in this series include:

The E-Myth Plumber
The E-Myth Women
The E-Myth Experience
Learn more at www.michaelegerberpartners.com

Have you created an E-Myth enterprise? Would you like to become a co-author of an E-Myth book in your industry? Go to www.michaelegerberpartners.com

THE MICHAEL E. GERBER
ENTREPRENEUR'S LIBRARY
It keeps growing . . .

Thank you for reading another E-Myth Expert book.

Who do you know who is an expert in their industry?

Who has applied The E-Myth to the improvement of their business as
Austin Clark has?

Who can add immense value to others in his or her industry
by sharing what he or she has learned?

Please share this book with that individual and share
that individual with us.

We at Michael E. Gerber Companies are determined to transform the
state of small business and entrepreneurship worldwide.
You can help.

To find out more, e-mail us at Michael E. Gerber Partners,
at gerber@michaelegerber.com.

To find out how *YOU* can apply the E-Myth to *YOUR* business, contact
us at www.michaelegerberpartners.com .

Thank you for living your Dream and changing the world.

Michael E. Gerber Partners
A Division of Michael E. Gerber Companies
Michael E. Gerber, Chairman, Co-Founder
Michael E. Gerber Companies™
Creator of The E-Myth Evolution™
P.O. Box 131195, Carlsbad, CA 92013
gerber@michaelegerber.com
www.michaelegerbercompanies.com

Join The Evolution ^{SM}

Find the latest updates:
www.MichaelEGerberCompanies.com
www.facebook.com/MichaelEGerberCo
www.linkedin.com/company/michael-e.-gerber-companies/

New Programs:
https://RadicalU.com/
www.TheNewDreamingRoom.com

Follow & Subscribe Michael E. Gerber:
www.linkedin.com/in/michaelegerber
www.youtube.com/michaelegerber
www.twitter.com/michaelegerber
www.instagram.com/michaelegerber/

Join Michael's Private Facebook Group:
www.facebook.com/groups/BeyondEMyth/

Follow & Subscribe to Mrs. E-Myth – Luz Delia Gerber
www.linkedin.com/in/luzdeliagerber
www.facebook.com/LuzDeliaGerberAuthor/
www.twitter.com/luzdeliagerber
www.instagram.com/luzdeliagerber

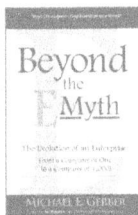

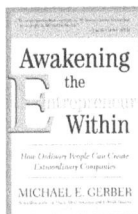

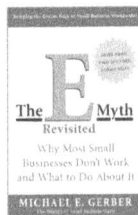

www.ingramcontent.com/pod-product-compliance
Lightning Source LLC
Chambersburg PA
CBHW031401180326
41458CB00043B/6565/J